Contents

Series Preface   vi

Preface   vii

Contributors   ix

Chapter 1   Children's Physical Activity Patterns: **1**
The Implications for Physical Education
  —Neil Armstrong

Physical Activity and the Prevention of
    Coronary Heart Disease   1
British Children's Habitual Physical Activity   4
The Implications for Children's Physical Education   9
References   14

Chapter 2   Promoting Health in Primary School   **17**
Physical Education
  —Mike Sleap

Health as an Objective for Physical Education   17
The Importance of Promoting Health in Primary School
    Physical Education   21
Review of Initiatives Emphasizing Health as an Objective for
    Primary Physical Education   23
The Happy Heart Project   29
Final Comments   33
References   33

Chapter 3   Physical Education and the National Curriculum   **37**
  —John Alderson and David Crutchley

Issues Facing Physical Education in the Development
    of a National Curriculum Statement   38
A Rationale for Physical Education in the National Curriculum   43
Aim and Long-Term Objectives of Physical Education   54
The General Pattern of the Physical Education Curriculum 5
    Through 16   55

The Extracurricular Programme in Physical Education 60
Conclusion 61
Appendix: Studies on the Value of Physical Education 61
References 62

Chapter 4 **Physical Education and Sport: The Interface**   **63**
    —Elizabeth B. Murdoch

The Substitution Model 64
The Versus Model 66
The Reinforcement Model 67
The Sequence Model 69
An Integration Model 71
References 76

Chapter 5 **New Directions in Games Teaching**   **79**
    —Rod Thorpe

Games in the Physical Education Programme 80
Extracurricular Games 88
The Games Experience in the Curriculum 91
Teaching for Understanding 92
A Games Education 95
Summary 97
References 98

Chapter 6 **Equal Opportunities and Physical Education**   **101**
    —Margaret Talbot

Equal Treatment 102
Equal Outcomes 103
Egalitarianism 104
Equal Opportunity 105
Three Stages of Problem Solving 109
Dimensions of Change 110
Nature of Professionalism 111
A Widening Knowledge Gap 115
Gatekeeping in Physical Education 115
Confronting Discrimination 116
Conclusion 117
References 118

Chapter 7 **Physical Education for Children With Severe**   **121**
    Learning Difficulties
    —Michael Alcott

Introduction 121
Current Practice 124

**Physical Education Association
of Great Britain and Northern Ireland**

New

Human Kinetics Books

Library of Congress Cataloging-in-Publication Data

New directions in physical education / Neil Armstrong, editor ;
   Physical Education Association of Great Britain and Northern
   Ireland.
      p.   cm.
   Includes bibliographical references.
   ISBN 0-87322-294-6
   1. Physical education and training--Study and teaching--Great
Britain.   2. Physical education for children--Study and teaching-
-Great Britain.   I. Armstrong, Neil.   II. Physical Education
Association of Great Britain and Northern Ireland.
GV365.5.G7N49   1990   90-31892
613.7'1'0941--dc20   CIP

British Library Cataloguing in Publication Data
New directions in physical education.
   Vol.1-
   1. Physical education
   I. Physical Education Association of Great Britain and
   Northern Ireland
   613.7

ISBN: 0-87322-294-6
ISSN: 1048-6224

Developmental Editor: Holly Gilly
Copyeditor: Peter Nelson
Assistant Editors: Valerie Hall, Timothy
            Ryan, Robert King
Proofreader: Pam Johnson
Production Director: Ernie Noa

Typesetters: Yvonne Winsor, Brad Colson
Text Design: Keith Blomberg
Text Layout: Kimberlie Henris
Cover Design: Jack Davis
Text Illustrations: Denise Lowry
Printer: Versa Press

Printed in the United States of America

10 9 8 7 6 5 4 3 2 1

Human Kinetics Publishers (UK), Ltd.
P.O. Box 18
Rawdon, Leeds, England LS19 6TG
(0532) 504211

U.S. Office:
Human Kinetics Publishers, Inc.
Box 5076, Champaign, IL 61825-5076
1-800-747-4HKP

Some Suggestions   130
Final Word   133
Appendix: Definitions of Conditions Associated
    With Severe Learning Difficulties   134
References   134

Chapter 8   Examinations and Assessment   **137**
in Physical Education
    —Robert Carroll

Examinations   138
Records of Achievement and Profiling   151
Conclusion   156
Appendix: Examining Bodies   157
References   158

Index   161

Series Preface

New Directions in Physical Education is a Physical Education Association Research Centre initiative to be published annually on behalf of the Physical Education Association of Great Britain and Northern Ireland.

It is envisaged that each edition of *New Directions in Physical Education* will include relevant contributions from recognized leaders in the field of physical education on topics of current interest in sport, dance, and physical, health, and outdoor education. Contributors to the present volume were selected by the editor, and, of course, the views expressed are those of the authors and not necessarily those of the Physical Education Association of Great Britain and Northern Ireland. Suggestions of suitable topics worthy of inclusion in future volumes and of potential contributors would be welcomed by the editor and the recently established Editorial Board. Correspondence should be addressed directly to Neil Armstrong, PEA Research Centre, School of Education, University of Exeter, Exeter, EX1 2LU, United Kingdom.

Preface

In the opening chapter of this volume, Neil Armstrong outlines some of the data on children's physical activity patterns that have emerged from the Coronary Prevention in Children Project. He concludes that children have surprisingly low levels of physical activity and discusses the implications of this finding for the physical education curriculum. Mike Sleap argues that the promotion of health is a 'core' objective of physical education in primary schools. He describes the development of a primary school health promotion programme and emphasizes the importance of fashioning an environment where the primary school child has every opportunity to be active and stay active.

Alderson and Crutchley examine the physical education programme in the context of developing and implementing a National Curriculum. Somewhat controversially, they conclude that they would be happy to see the subject labelled 'sport' or 'sport studies'. Elizabeth Murdoch continues the debate by analysing a series of models that have arisen from the ways in which the interface between the two distinct phenomena of sport and physical education has been perceived. She proposes an integration model based on partnership between sport and physical education. In the following chapter Rod Thorpe initially focuses on the current debate about the place of games in the physical education programme. He then considers the sort of games education that might provide a sound educational experience in its own right and a base from which to move into sport at any level.

Margaret Talbot addresses the key issue of equal opportunity in physical education. She emphasizes that physical education should be structured in such a way that all children are encouraged to enjoy physical movement on their own terms and to develop confidence, assertiveness and control over their bodies. Michael Alcott looks at physical education in schools for pupils with severe learning difficulties. He identifies the range of pupils and legislation relating to them, outlines current provision, and then suggests how the physical education of children with severe learning difficulties could be enhanced. In the final chapter Bob Carroll overviews the complex field of examinations and assessment in physical education and relates the current situation to such recent developments as the introduction of a National Curriculum with physical education as a foundation subject.

The publication of this volume would not have been possible without the tremendous support of the authors, the publishers and the staff of both the headquarters of the Physical Education Association and the Physical Education Association Research Centre. My thanks to all concerned.

Neil Armstrong, PhD, FPEA
University of Exeter
United Kingdom

Contributors

Michael Alcott
Deputy Headteacher
Green Hedges School
Stapleford
Cambridge CB2 5BJ

John Alderson, PhD
Reader in Recreation
Sheffield City Polytechnic
36 Collegiate Crescent
Sheffield S10 2BP

Neil Armstrong, PhD, FPEA
Senior Lecturer in Education
Director of the PEA Research Centre
University of Exeter
Exeter EX1 2LU

Robert Carroll
Lecturer in Physical Education
Department of Education
University of Manchester
Manchester M13 9PL

David Crutchley
Principal Lecturer in Recreation
Sheffield City Polytechnic
36 Collegiate Crescent
Sheffield S10 2BP

Elizabeth B. Murdoch, FPEA
Head of School
Chelsea School of Human Movement
Brighton Polytechnic
Eastbourne BN20 7SP

Mike Sleap
Lecturer in Education
Department of Education
University of Hull
Hull HU5 2EH

Margaret Talbot, FPEA
Professor of Physical Education
Carnegie Department of Physical Education
Leeds Polytechnic
Leeds LS1 3HE

Rod Thorpe
Senior Lecturer in Physical Education
Department of Physical Education and Sports Science
University of Technology
Loughborough LE11 3TU

Chapter 1

Children's Physical Activity Patterns: The Implications for Physical Education

Neil Armstrong

The case for increased physical activity can be argued across a wide spectrum (see Fentem, Bassey, and Turnbull, 1988), but in this chapter I will focus on the evidence that links habitual physical activity with the prevention of coronary heart disease (CHD). I will describe the recent findings on British children's habitual physical activity that have emerged from the Coronary Prevention in Children Project, then discuss the implications of the research results for the community, the family and the physical education profession.

Physical Activity and the Prevention of Coronary Heart Disease

Jerry Morris and his colleagues (Morris, Heady, Raffle, Roberts, & Parks, 1953) were the first to attract serious attention to the hypothesis that physical inactivity may be related to CHD. Morris studied CHD in 31,000 London Transport workers, comparing the drivers with the more active conductors on double-decker buses. The conductors had a 50% lower rate of heart attacks than the drivers, and drivers suffered twice as many fatal heart attacks as conductors. The findings of the study were, however, subsequently criticized on the basis of self-selection of occupation. Further, Morris's own analysis (Morris, Heady, & Raffle, 1956) confirmed that the conductors were more lightly built than the drivers, a difference that was present from the time of taking up employment with London Transport. Nevertheless, Morris's pioneering work stimulated the initiation of numerous epidemiological investigations into the effects of occupational activity on CHD.

Inverse patterns of physical activity and CHD risk were found between letter carriers and mail clerks, farmers and sedentary townsfolk, workers on different jobs in kibbutzim in Israel, railroad sorting yard workers and clerks, and San

Francisco longshoremen loading cargo into ship holds or tallying it into warehouses. Contrasting or inconsistent results, however, were found in comparisons of Los Angeles civil servants, Chicago industrial workers and Finnish lumberjacks. These 'occupational activity studies' have been extensively reviewed (e.g. Froelicher and Oberman, 1972; Milvy, Forbes, and Brown, 1977) and have been criticized on several accounts. The major criticisms include the self-selection of subjects, the inadequacy of CHD classification (i.e. the combination of infarcts and angina into a single CHD score) and the inability of broad job categorization to adequately distinguish between levels of physical activity.

Paffenbarger's 22-year study of 3,686 California longshoremen (recently analysed by Paffenbarger himself, 1988) is probably the best controlled and least open to the stated criticisms of the occupational studies. Job categories were carefully defined according to union agreements that required all employees to be highly active cargo handlers for at least their first 5 years of employment. Most men did heavy work much longer, 13 years on average, and shifted to less physically demanding jobs for reasons not of health but of higher pay and prestige. Paffenbarger argued that these work practices suggest that any differences in CHD rate for longshoremen in high- or low-activity groups could not be accounted for by self-selection alone or by job transfers that might have accompanied premonitory symptoms of impending heart problems. Physical activity patterns were verified by on-the-job energy output measurements, although cardiorespiratory fitness was not checked. Shifts in job assignments were noted annually, occupational activity was recorded in kilocalories per week, and mortality rates were derived from official death certificates and man-years of observation. Multivariate analyses, incorporating cigarette consumption and systolic blood pressure as independent variables, suggested that the risk of a heart attack was about twice as great in longshoremen whose work demanded a low energy expenditure as in those with a high energy expenditure classification.

By the 1960s it had become apparent that if physical activity was to contribute to the prevention of CHD, it would have to be predominantly through leisure time activity because mechanization and automation had reduced physical activity in the workplace. The research teams headed by Morris and Paffenbarger were again at the forefront of developments. Morris and his colleagues (reviewed in Morris, Everitt, and Semmence, 1987) undertook an extensive 8.5-year prospective study of leisure activities in a group of about 17,000 men in the executive grade of the British civil service. They found that those who reported vigorous leisure time physical activity had a CHD rate less than half of those who reported a lack of such activity. Paffenbarger's group (reviewed in 1988) completed an equally extensive study, following almost 17,000 Harvard University graduates, that related both certified causes of death and incidence of physician-diagnosed CHD to smoking habits and continued participation in various forms of physical activity. Analysis of the data demonstrated that current and continuing adequate physical activity, rather than only a history of youthful vigour and athleticism, was inversely associated with risk of CHD in all age brackets studied.

The results of Paffenbarger's and Morris's research on the relationship between leisure time activity and CHD have been supported by numerous other studies. Recent critical reviews of the literature (e.g. Shephard, 1986; Siscovick, LaPorte, and Newman, 1985) have concluded that physically active individuals are at a lower risk for CHD than less active persons, but reservations concerning experimental design have been expressed. It is unfortunate that there have been few studies involving women as subjects. The results with women have been generally inconclusive, possibly because fewer women develop the disease before old age and the numbers are too small for significant results to emerge (Fentem, Bassey, & Turnbull, 1988). Nevertheless, a recent, authoritative meta-analysis (Powell, Thompson, Casperson, & Kendrick, 1987) focused on all papers published in the English language that provide sufficient data to calculate relative risk or odds ratios for CHD at different levels of physical activity. The meta-analysis concluded that

> the inverse association between physical activity and incidence of CHD is consistently observed, especially in the better designed studies; this association is appropriately sequenced, biologically graded, plausible, and coherent with existing knowledge. Therefore, the observations reported in the literature support the inference that physical activity is inversely and causally related to the incidence of CHD. (p. 283)

It seems that activity needs to be current to be beneficial and that habitual physical activity using large muscle groups for sustained periods of time is the only form of activity consistently and substantially associated with a lower incidence of CHD. Heartbeat Wales (1987) summarized the current research evidence as follows:

> For heart health an energy expenditure of the order of 300 kcal per day in excess of sedentary requirements is needed. This should be performed at an intensity of more than 7.5 kcal per minute and at a frequency of three times per week. In practical terms a minimum of 20/30 minutes of exercise (of at least brisk walking intensity) three times a week is recommended as a contribution towards the prevention of coronary heart disease. (p. 3)

An intensity of 7.5 kcal/min (31.5 kJ/min) is of a lower intensity than that normally prescribed in an aerobic exercise programme and approximates to only about 70% of maximal heart rate. Paffenbarger, in his studies of Harvard alumni, placed less emphasis on how vigorous the activity was, and he was more concerned with total energy output but, as Morris et al. (1987) pointed out, Paffenbarger reported more positive effects in men who undertook vigorous activity.

An active way of life appears to prevent or delay CHD, but, despite a vast research effort, there is no clear understanding of the mechanisms involved. It is generally agreed that appropriate physical activity has positive effects on coronary risk factors. Other plausible mechanisms include improved cardiorespiratory efficiency, increased fibrinolytic activity, reduced platelet aggregation, reduced coronary thrombosis, increased resistance to ventricular fibrillation, increased myocardial vascularity and increased coronary artery size. The available evidence is, however, equivocal, and several of these beneficial adaptations have yet to be convincingly demonstrated in human subjects. Nevertheless, although the debate over the precise underlying mechanisms may continue, the circumstantial evidence amassed by epidemiological studies and the known cardiovascular benefits of physical activity justify the present emphasis on CHD prevention through the medium of physical activity.

British Children's Habitual Physical Activity

Recognizing that the origins of many degenerative diseases (including CHD) are embedded in patterns of behaviour developed during childhood, the United States Department of Health and Human Services (1980) decreed that one of the health objectives for the nation is that 'by 1990, the proportion of children and adolescents aged 10 to 17 participating regularly in appropriate physical activities, particularly cardiorespiratory fitness programs which can be carried into adulthood, should be greater than 90 percent' (p. 80).

'Appropriate physical activity' refers to the minimum frequency, duration and intensity with which an individual must participate in physical activity to maintain an effectively functioning cardiorespiratory system. Regular, vigorous and prolonged physical activity is generally accepted as essential for an effectively functioning cardiorespiratory system. The definition adopted by the United States National Children and Youth Fitness Study referred to 'exercise involving large muscle groups in dynamic movement for periods of 20 minutes or longer, three or more times weekly, at an intensity requiring 60 percent or more of an individual's cardiorespiratory capacity' (Ross & Gilbert, 1985, p. 49). This definition appears to satisfy most expert recommendations and, with children, refers to activities that elicit heart rates equal to or in excess of 140 beats/min (approximately 70% of maximum heart rate). This is in close agreement with research findings that relate activity to CHD prevention in adults.

How many British children experience three 20-minute periods per week in which they sustain their heart rates above 139 beats/min? The available literature is relatively scarce and beset with problems of interpretation caused by the inherent difficulty of determining the quality and quantity of children's physical activity. Reliable data are limited and need to be interpreted in relation to the methodology employed. For example, self-assessment, through retrospective questionnaires or daily diaries, of the intensity and duration of periods of activity by children is especially problematic because children are less time-conscious than adults and tend to engage in physical activity at sporadic times and intensities. Ideally, the relative intensity and duration of activities should be simultaneously measured, and if a true picture of habitual activity is required, at least three days of monitoring are necessary. The technique used must be socially acceptable, it should not burden the child with cumbersome equipment, and it should minimally influence the child's normal physical activity pattern. Before the Coronary Prevention in Children Project, no survey of British children's habitual physical activity that satisfied these criteria had been carried out.

We utilized a self-contained, computerized telemetry system, the Sport Tester 3000, to continuously record the minute-by-minute heart rate of over 300 children. The Sport Tester 3000 (Figure 1.1) consists of a lightweight transmitter, fixed to the chest with electrodes, and a receiver and microcomputer, worn as a watch on the wrist. It has been found to be a reliable and valid means of recording heart rates with children; a recent survey of the most popular commercially available heart rate monitors (Leger & Thivierge, 1988) concluded that the Sport Tester 3000 was first choice because 'in addition to having excellent validity and stability it permits almost total freedom of motion'. The Sport Tester is capable of storing minute-by-minute heart rates for up to 16 hours. If it is interfaced with a microcomputer, the development of a simple programme allows sustained periods with heart rates above 139 beats/min (BPM) (appropriate physical activity) to be readily identified and recorded.

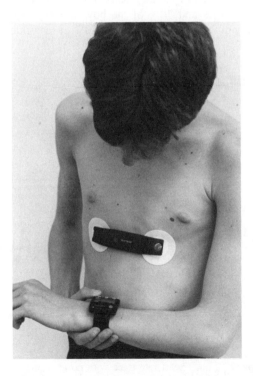

Figure 1.1 A child fitted with a Sport Tester 3000 heart rate telemetry system.

During the initial phase of the Coronary Prevention in Children Project, we randomly selected a group of children from the total sample to participate in a substudy concerned with monitoring heart rates on a daily basis. A transmitter and electrodes were fitted to each child's chest, and a receiver was strapped around the wrist. The monitoring period lasted from about 9.00 a.m. until 9.00 p.m. The receivers were retrieved the following morning, and the data were analysed. Typical heart rate traces are illustrated in Figures 1.2 and 1.3. The children were refitted with Sport Testers, and the process was repeated over three weekdays. Three-day traces were obtained on 63 girls (mean age 13.7 years) and 34 boys (mean age 13.3 years). The mean percentage of time spent in each heart rate range is illustrated in Figure 1.4. On average the boys spent only 6.7% of their time during the monitored period with heart rates above 139 BPM (appropriate physical activity). The girls spent significantly less time, only 4.3%, with heart rates in this range. The interpretation of continuous heart rate data, however, is complex because heart rate not only reflects the metabolism of the child but also the transient emotional state, the prevailing climatic conditions and the specific muscle groups that perform the activity. The primary consideration should there-fore be the number and length of sustained periods of appropriate physical activity rather than the total time in specified heart rate bands (see Figure 1.3).

Over 85% of the girls and 70% of the boys did not even sustain a single 20-minute period with their heart rates above 70% of maximum. Only two boys

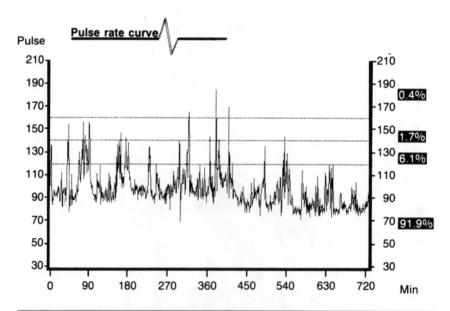

Figure 1.2   A typical 12-hour heart rate trace with no appropriate physical activity.

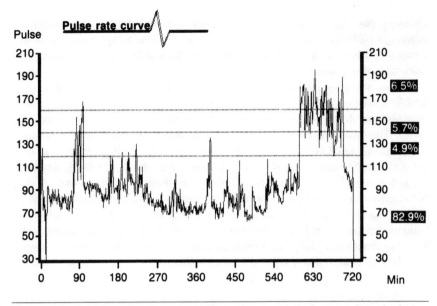

Figure 1.3 A 12-hour heart rate trace illustrating a period of appropriate physical activity.

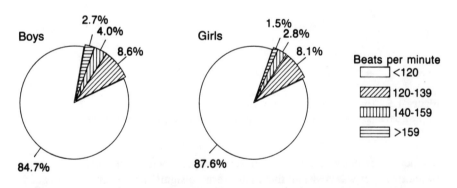

Figure 1.4 The mean percentage of time spent in each heart rate range during 3 days of daytime monitoring (boys, mean age 13.3 years; girls, mean age 13.7 years).

and none of the girls achieved three 20-minute periods with their heart rates above 139 BPM. Fifty per cent of the girls failed to achieve a 10-minute period of appropriate physical activity, and 2 of the boys and 11 of the girls did not even manage to sustain a single 5-minute period with their heart rates above 139 BPM.

The boys spent significantly more 5-minute and 10-minute periods with heart rates above 139 BPM than the girls. To put these figures into perspective, it is worth noting that brisk walking (6 to 8 km per hr) on the treadmill elicited steady state heart rates in excess of 139 BPM with the same group of children.

Another substudy involved primary school children, from the same distinct catchment area, who were monitored in exactly the same manner. Three-day traces were obtained from 24 girls (mean age 10.6 years) and 18 boys (mean age 10.6 years). The mean percentage of time spent in each heart rate band is illustrated in Figure 1.5. Only about 30% of this group of young children managed to sustain a single 20-minute period with their heart rates above 139 BPM, and only one girl achieved three 20-minute periods at this intensity. Twenty-five per cent of the girls and 17% of the boys failed to sustain a single 10-minute period of appropriate physical activity in 3 days, but only one boy failed to achieve a 5-minute period at this level. There were no significant differences between the boys and the girls in daily heart rate responses or in sustained 5- or 10-minute periods with heart rates above 70% of maximum.

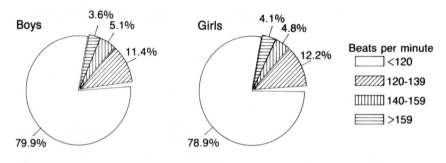

Figure 1.5   The mean percentage of time spent in each heart rate range during 3 days of daytime monitoring (boys, mean age 10.6 years; girls, mean age 10.6 years).

When the primary school children were compared with their secondary school counterparts, it was revealed that there were no significant differences between the relevant heart rate responses of the two groups of boys. However, the secondary school girls displayed significantly fewer 5-minute and 10-minute periods with heart rates above 139 BPM and significantly less total time in this range than the primary school girls. Monitoring the heart rates of the same children on a Saturday demonstrated that all groups were even less active during the weekend than during the week.

Our data, the first to be generated from British children, indicate that children have surprisingly low levels of physical activity and that many children seldom experience the intensity and duration of physical activity associated with a lower incidence of CHD in adults. The activity level of teenage girls appears to be a particular problem. When the results are related to the marked decrease in activity with age that recent self-report surveys of adults appear to have identified in the United Kingdom (e.g. Heartbeat Wales, 1987), the magnitude of the problem becomes readily apparent.

The Implications for Children's Physical Education

The Community

Public awareness of the importance of increasing children's physical activity patterns needs to be raised; we have found local radio stations to be very willing to co-operate in doing this. Attractive and accessible sports facilities need to be made available at reasonable cost and at times when children can use them, such as during weekends and school holidays (School Sport Forum, 1988). Yet, at a time when local authorities and local education authorities should be extending multiple use of their facilities, evidence is accumulating to support the view that the problem of maintenance of facilities and resources for physical education is becoming serious (Physical Education Association, 1987). Lack of opportunity to participate has not been identified as a major factor in the Coronary Prevention in Children Project, but many of the children we have studied have emphasized the value of a family approach to encouraging activity. They have particularly highlighted the importance of parental and sibling example. Attitudes towards physical activity are established at an early age; parents therefore have a prime responsibility to encourage their children to engage in active play, both spontaneous and formal, but the community must provide adequate safe, clean play areas for this to take place.

The Family

The value of parents as significant socializing agents influencing sport and activity involvement has been confirmed in several other studies. Family encouragement and the involvement of parents in vigorous activity have been found to be instrumental in the involvement of children, and parental attitudes towards activity have been shown to demonstrate a significant effect upon children's intentions to exercise (see Sallis and Nader, 1988, for a review).

Perhaps the origins of the remarkably low physical activity patterns of teenage girls lie in parental attitudes because parental behaviour appears to be more influential for increase in exercise frequency among girls than boys. Parents elicit gross-motor behaviour at a young age more from their sons than their daughters. Because exercise and sport have been sex-stereotyped as masculine in our culture, boys have more parental reinforcement for exercise than girls. Boys' games are generally of longer duration, and the ceiling of skill is often higher. The type of game normally adopted by boys can be played in more simple versions at younger ages, becoming more challenging with age as higher levels of skill and strategy are incorporated. In contrast, the types of games often adopted by girls seem to be less challenging with increasing age because the ceiling of skill was achieved at an earlier age (see Lewko and Greendorfer, 1982, and Gottlieb and Chen, 1985, for reviews). Parents should be encouraged to provide positive role models for their children's activity behaviour, and parental modeling may be especially important for girls.

The School

The primary school provides an ideal environment in which to further promote active lifestyles in partnership with the home. Children's natural curiosity can be used to help them understand how their bodies function, and the importance of physical activity can be emphasized and related to other aspects of education. The introduction of the National Curriculum invites primary school teachers to explore possibilities for developing aspects of the core subjects. This opportunity, in the present context, has been clearly recognized and illustrated in *Science in the National Curriculum* (National Curriculum Council, 1989).

Young children can be guided through a physical education curriculum that includes gymnastics, games skills, dance, swimming, athletics and outdoor education, with plenty of opportunities to explore the full range of available activities. With a balanced, enjoyable programme, children can develop a repertoire of motor skills, achieve success at their own levels, and feel confident enough in their own abilities to want to pursue more active lifestyles. Leisure time activity can be encouraged by making equipment (e.g. skipping ropes and balls) available at playtimes. Holiday activities and the availability of local clubs and facilities can be brought to children's attention, in an attempt to promote positive attitudes to physical activity.

The recent Sports Council publication *School Sport Forum* (1988) advocates 'a daily session of vigorous activity in each primary school as part of the physical education programme or as a supplement to it', but this recommendation needs to be viewed with caution because children's resistance to participation in compulsory, structured programmes of vigorous physical activity is well documented (e.g. Cooper et al., 1975). It is much more important to make children's early activity experiences enjoyable in order to foster future participation.

In the secondary school it would be wrong to divorce physical activity from other aspects of a healthy lifestyle, so special provision needs to be made for a cross-curricular approach to activity education. Science, home economics, physical education, health education, school meals and school nursing staff should all be involved in a multidisciplinary, integrated approach. The emergence of the National Curriculum has provided a useful framework for projects of this nature. Physical education staff must grasp the opportunity to contribute to the many relevant areas discussed in *Science in the National Curriculum* (National Curriculum Council, 1989). Relevant parts of the programmes of study should be interpreted with the emphasis on the promotion of active lifestyles that will persist into adult life.

Physical education by its very nature is the ideal medium for promoting physical activity, and physical education teachers have reacted positively to the recent emergence of health-related fitness in the curriculum. A survey by the Physical Education Association (PEA) (1987) illustrated the increased importance teachers now give to health-related fitness as a major objective of the physical education programme. The same survey, however, reported that traditional team games continue to dominate the programme and pointed out that Her Majesty's Inspectorate (HMI) Reports have both emphasized the imbalance that such a limited physical education experience may create and noted that there is a tendency for an overindulgence in games where supervision rather than dynamic teaching is in evidence. An HMI recently commented that 'we spend hundreds of hours teaching the skills of the major team games when in fact the vast majority of youngsters will not actively pursue these activities once they leave school' (Dowling, 1987, p. 15).

In fact, many children are discouraged from participating much earlier than this, perhaps through lack of competitive success simply due to their biological clocks running at different rates from those of their classmates. My colleague John Balding (1988) asked 18,000 children, through the well-established Health-Related Behaviour Questionnaire, whether they had participated in various activities at least once per week outside school curriculum time. As expected, soccer was identified as the most popular sport with boys, but participation fell from 58.6% of first-year boys to 41.8% of fifth-year boys. The other major game for boys, rugby, had a participation rate that fell from 15.3% to only 6.3% over the same time period. On the other hand, 44.8% of first-year boys played snooker at least once per week, and by the fifth year it had replaced soccer as the most popular sport. With girls, netball participation was reported to fall from a mere 19.4% of first-year girls to only 6.3% of fifth-year girls. Hockey participation fell from an even more dismal 10.1% to 5.7% over the same age range, yet the PEA survey revealed that heads of girls' physical education departments attached more importance, in terms of time allocated, to team games than any other area of the curriculum throughout the 5 years of secondary schooling. These figures lend strong support to the belief that competitive team games are of relatively little interest to the majority of adolescent girls. It therefore seems that although physical education teachers perceive the importance of promoting active lifestyles, their curricula may not be geared towards achieving this objective.

Fitness Testing

Within time allocated to health-related fitness, it appears that large chunks are devoted to 'fitness' testing. Yet, the quantitative assessment of children's physical fitness is one of the most complex problems in exercise science. Furthermore, health-related fitness tests that are suitable for use in the school environment and that provide valid and objective measures of fitness are not available. All performance tests (e.g. sit-ups, shuttle runs, the flexed arm hang) are primarily dependent upon the subject's motivation to do well, and several of the most popular tests are not even based on sound physiological foundations. Many of the data generated by these tests are therefore more likely to cause confusion than analyse physical fitness or clarify relevant health-related concepts. The sensitivity of the components of health-related fitness to exercise is largely dependent upon maturation and genetic endowment; because each child grows and develops at his or her own rate, it is extremely difficult to separate the contributions of growth, maturation and exercise to any observed changes in performance (see Armstrong, 1987 and 1989, for detailed critiques).

Cardiorespiratory fitness at a particular point in time can be assessed in an accredited laboratory (Hale et al., 1989). It is widely recognized that the maximal rate at which oxygen can be consumed during exercise with large muscle groups (maximal oxygen uptake, or $\dot{V}O_2$max) is the best single indicator of cardiorespiratory fitness (Åstrand & Rodahl, 1986). We determined the $\dot{V}O_2$max (or peak $\dot{V}O_2$) of over 200 children, aged 11 to 15 years, by running them to exhaustion on a treadmill and simultaneously monitoring their cardiorespiratory responses to the exercise (see Armstrong and Davies, 1984, for an explanation of the difference between $\dot{V}O_2$max and peak $\dot{V}O_2$ in children). Our results demonstrated that the boys were as 'fit' as the first boys ever to have their cardiorespiratory fitness scientifically assessed in a laboratory over 50 years ago. More detailed comparisons of our data with results from elsewhere have shown that British children are as fit as children from similar environments and that there is no scientific evidence to support the premise that the cardiorespiratory fitness of children has deteriorated over time. When we compared children's cardiorespiratory fitness with their habitual physical activity, however, we found no relationship between the two—and it is current physical activity, not cardiorespiratory fitness, which most epidemiological studies have related to coronary prevention.

Fitness tests simply determine the obvious, at best only distinguishing the mature child from the immature child. The use of norm tables confounds the issue of relative fitness because tables constructed on the basis of chronological age cannot logically be used to classify individual children at different levels of skeletal and biological maturity. Moreover, having different norms for boys and girls results in different expectations. Norms are based on performances rather than capabilities; if teachers accept lower norms for girls as reflecting acceptable performance, girls will tend to meet these lower expectations (see Thomas and Thomas, 1988, for a review). Any attempt to introduce fitness testing as a means of assessing levels of attainment in physical education should therefore be strongly resisted.

Motivating Students

It must be demonstrated clearly to children that activity can be enjoyable and that competition or athletic excellence is not necessary for the promotion of health. Children need to be exposed to a wide variety of individual, partner and team activities, and the emphasis should be placed upon developing a sound foundation of motor skills that can contribute to successful and enjoyable activity experiences in both the present and the future. Motivations vary; for example, despite recent progress in female emancipation, 'looking better' remains a prime motivator for girls' participation in relevant activity (Shephard & Godin, 1986). The activity and leisure preferences of children and adults of different races and of different physical and intellectual capabilities are varied. These preferences need to be taken into consideration when designing a relevant curriculum.

Although the provision of a high activity content should be an important component of most physical education lessons, the prime objective underpinning the inclusion of health-related activity in the physical education curriculum should be for children to achieve 'activity independence'. Teachers must help and encourage children to internalize the motivation to be active so that when the extrinsic motivation of the teacher is removed, the child will continue with an active lifestyle. To achieve 'activity independence', children should understand the principles underlying healthy activity and be taught how to become informed decision makers who can plan and implement individual activity programmes that can be periodically reappraised and modified as they get older.

If teachers are to develop successful courses, they need to understand current concepts in exercise and health science and be cognizant of the growing body of knowledge associated with exercise adherence (see Dishman, 1988, for a review). This has far-reaching implications for both initial and continuing teacher education programmes.

Higher Education

Universities and other institutes of higher education must provide initial teacher-training students with a thorough grounding in both the practical and the theoretical aspects of exercise and health science. The potential cross-curricular contribution of physical education to the whole 5-to-16 curriculum must be emphasized, and suitable programmes of study must be integrated into current initial training courses. These courses should be underpinned and enriched with dynamic research programmes. In comparison to what we know about adults, we know very little about paediatric exercise and health science. Groups of scholars need to collaborate to address the exciting research problems on an interdisciplinary basis. Optimum methods of delivery of courses, founded on research results, urgently need to be investigated. Universities, colleges, local education authorities, and schools need to work together to design appropriate postgraduate courses and to encourage school-based action research in exercise and health science as part of the continuing professional development of experienced teachers.

The current level and pattern of children's physical activity is a cause for grave concern. Physical educators at all levels of education must collaborate with each other and with the community and the home to meet this challenge. The future health of our children depends upon it.

Acknowledgement

The data referred to in this paper were collected in collaboration with my colleagues John Balding, Peter Gentle and Brian Kirby of the Coronary Prevention in Children Research Group at the University of Exeter. Technical support was provided by Clive Williams, Pat Bond, Jenny Frost, Alison Husband and Joanne Williams. The studies were supported by grants from the Northcott Devon Medical Foundation, the Oxenham Will Trust and the IBM (UK) Trust.

References

Armstrong, N. (1987). A critique of fitness testing. In S. Biddle (Ed.), *Foundations of health-related fitness in physical education* (pp. 136-138). London: Ling.

Armstrong, N. (1989). Is fitness testing either valid or useful? *British Journal of Physical Education*, **20**, 66-67.

Armstrong, N., & Davies, B. (1984). The physiological and metabolic responses of children to exercise. *Physical Education Review*, **7**, 90-105.

Åstrand, P.O., & Rodahl, K. (1986). *A textbook of work physiology*. New York: McGraw-Hill.

Balding, J. (1988). *Young people in 1987*. Exeter: HEA Schools Health Education Unit.

Cooper, K.H., Purdy, J.G., Friedman, A., Bohannon, R.L., Harris, R.A., & Arends, J.A. (1975). An aerobics conditioning programme for the Fort Worth, TX, school district. *Research Quarterly*, **46**, 345-350.

Department of Health and Human Services. (1980). *Promoting health/preventing disease: Objectives for the nation* (DHEW [PMS] Publication No. 79-55071). Washington, DC: U.S. Government Printing Office.

Dishman, R.K. (1988). *Exercise adherence*. Champaign, IL: Human Kinetics.

Dowling, F. (1987). A health focus within physical education. In S. Biddle (Ed.), *Foundations of health-related fitness in physical education* (pp. 13-18). London: Ling.

Fentem, P.H., Bassey, E.J., & Turnbull, N.B. (1988). *The new case for exercise*. London: Sports Council and Health Education Authority.

Froelicher, V.F., & Oberman, A. (1972). Analysis of epidemiological studies of physical inactivity as risk factor for coronary artery disease. *Progress in Cardiovascular Diseases*, **15**, 41-65.

Gottlieb, N.H., & Chen, M.S. (1985). Sociocultural correlates of childhood sporting activities: Their implications for heart health. *Society of Science and Medicine*, **21**(5), 533-539.

Hale, T., Armstrong, N., Hardman, A., Jakeman, P., Sharp, C., & Winter, E. (1989). *The physiological assessment of the elite competitor*. Leeds: British Association of Sports Sciences.

Heartbeat Wales. (1987). *Exercise for health* (Heartbeat Report No. 23). Cardiff: Author.

Leger, L., & Thivierge, M. (1988). Heart rate monitors: Validity, stability and functionality. *Physician and Sports Medicine*, **16**, 143-151.

Lewko, J.H., & Greendorfer, S.L. (1982). Family influences and sex differences in children's socialization into sport: A review. In R.A. Magill, M.J. Ash, & F.L. Smoll (Eds.), *Children in sport* (pp. 279-293). Champaign, IL: Human Kinetics.

Milvy, P., Forbes, W.F., & Brown, K.S. (1977). A critical review of epidemiological studies of physical activity. *Annals of the New York Academy of Science*, **301**, 519-549.

Morris, J.N., Everitt, M.G., & Semmence, A.M. (1987). Exercise and coronary heart disease. In D. Macleod, R. Maughan, M. Nimmo, T. Reilly, & C. Williams (Eds.), *Exercise benefits, limits and adaptations* (pp. 4-17). London: E and FN Spon.

Morris, J.N., Heady, J.A., & Raffle, P.A. (1956). Physique of London busmen: Epidemiology of uniforms. *Lancet*, **2**, 569-570.

Morris, J.N., Heady, J., Raffle, P., Roberts, C., & Parks, J. (1953). Coronary heart disease and physical activity of work. *Lancet*, **2**, 1053-1057, 1111-1120.

National Curriculum Council. (1989). *Science in the national curriculum*. London: Her Majesty's Stationery Office.

Paffenbarger, R.S. (1988). Contributions of epidemiology to exercise science and cardiovascular health. *Medicine and Science in Sports and Exercise*, **20**, 426-438.

Physical Education Association. (1987). *Physical education in schools*. London: Ling.

Powell, K.E., Thompson, P.D., Casperson, C.J., & Kendrick, J.S. (1987). Physical activity and the incidence of coronary heart disease. *Annual Reviews of Public Health*, **8**, 253-287.

Ross, J.G., & Gilbert, G.G. (1985). The National Children and Youth Fitness Study: A summary of findings. *Journal of Physical Education, Recreation and Dance*, **56**, 45-50.

Sallis, J.F., & Nader, P.R. (1988). Family determinants of health behaviours. In D.S. Gochman (Ed.), *Health behaviour* (pp. 107-123). New York: Plenum Press.

School Sport Forum. (1988). *Sport and young people*. London: Sports Council.

Shephard, R.J. (1986). Exercise in coronary heart disease. *Sports Medicine*, **3**, 26-49.

Shephard, R.J., & Godin, G. (1986). Behavioural intentions and activity of children. In J. Rutenfranz, R. Mocellin, & F. Klimt (Eds.), *Children and exercise XII* (pp. 103-109). Champaign, IL: Human Kinetics.

Siscovick, D.S., La Porte, R.E., & Newman, J.M. (1985). The disease-specific benefits and risks of physical activity and exercise. *Public Health Report*, **100**, 180-188.

Thomas, J.R., & Thomas, K.T. (1988). Development of gender differences in physical activity. *Quest*, **40**, 219-229.

Chapter 2

Promoting Health in Primary School Physical Education

Mike Sleap

It is widely accepted that regular physical activity does make a worthwhile contribution to an individual's health and in particular has a significant role to play in lessening the risk factors associated with heart disease (Åstrand, 1987). It is also recognized that a major proportion of the population does not engage in sufficient physical activity to derive these benefits to health (Powell, Spain, Christenson, & Mollenkamp, 1986). Although medical authorities have in the past encouraged people to take exercise, there are now signs that it is becoming a more serious public issue. Many writers have commented upon the disappointing impact of efforts aimed at promoting exercise amongst adults (Dishman & Dunn, 1988; McIntosh & Charlton, 1985). Therefore, new initiatives are being explored with children, which has led to the high profile of health-related fitness as a feature of school-based physical education.

Health as an Objective for Physical Education

Maintenance of health has always been important to physical educators. At the beginning of the twentieth century, physical education was dominated by this idea: 'The primary objective of any course of physical exercise in schools is to maintain, and if possible, improve the health and physique of the children' (Board of Education, 1905, p. 9).

This emphasis was dictated by the poor health of schoolchildren and the lack of fitness amongst youth who were needed for the armed forces. By the end of the Second World War, McIntosh (1972) noted, 'Drill had given place to therapy and therapy to self-discovery and body awareness' (p. 283). Concern for health was suppressed in recognition of improved general health and changed social conditions, which allowed other objectives to come to the fore (Yates, 1977). In the 1960s and the 1970s, attention was focused not only upon self-discovery but also upon the acquisition of physical skills and the potential of physical activities as lifelong leisure pursuits. In the 1980s growing anxiety about degenerative diseases shifted the emphasis again. Ironically, even though medical knowledge has greatly advanced and living conditions are much improved, physical education has turned full circle, with health once more appearing to be a major ideology. However, Williams (1988) has pointed out that there is a characteristic which distinguishes the current revival of health and fitness as a justification for physical education from earlier syllabuses underpinned by health considerations. Whereas pre-war physical education had a short-term therapeutic value, there is now much more of a concern for the development of 'lifelong patterns of physical activity' (Williams, 1988).

One of the most recent statements regarding the aims and objectives of physical education came in a report by McIntosh for the Inner London Education Authority. Two of the seven objectives listed there are pertinent to this discussion (McIntosh, 1988, p. 17):

- Encouraging physically active lifestyles
- Developing an understanding of exercise and its relationship to fitness and well-being

Reservations About the Role of Physical Education in Health Promotion

There can be no doubt about the health focus to physical education proposed in the McIntosh report. Nevertheless, there are some who would urge caution on this issue, and the following discussion concentrates upon four reservations expressed about the role of health as an objective for physical education.

'Naturalistic Fallacy'

First, McNamee (1988) has suggested that it is a 'naturalistic fallacy' to assert that physical education has a role to play in health. He added that, because there is empirical evidence regarding activity levels and hypokinetic diseases, it does not necessarily follow that physical education should have to do anything about it. It could be a problem for doctors, health clubs, health administrators or some other agency, but not specifically one for schools. It has to be admitted that the main curriculum development initiative on this topic, the Health and Physical Education Project (Dowling, 1986), has not really answered this criticism.

Perhaps the most convincing reason for promoting active lifestyles in schools is that given by Bar-Or (1987), who emphasized that the school was the only place where 'all' children, irrespective of background, sex, race and athletic prowess, have the opportunity to benefit from such an experience. Providing further support for his case, Bar-Or commented that the physical education teacher had been seen as the most suitable coordinator for a programme in the United States that had been effective in ameliorating weight problems in schoolchildren.

The similarity, and even overlap, between weight control and physical activity is obvious.

Some other points would also seem valid here. Efforts need to be directed at schoolchildren because adult behaviour has proven to be so resistant to change and it is clearly important to promote healthy lifestyles before heart disease risk factors start to build up. Physical education has often been viewed as education 'of' or education 'through' the physical (Munrow, 1972), but education 'about' the physical is surely just as important. Education about keeping the body in good condition to enhance the quality and quantity of life could well be considered as relevant as the teaching of a physical skill for a game which might never be played once school days are over.

'Conceptual Confusion'

A further problem, which has been promulgated by Colquhoun and Kirk (1987), is that there is a 'conceptual confusion' about the teaching of health in physical education. In Britain the subject matter of physical education has been determined mainly by staff within individual schools. Although there has usually been a common core of content, it is possible for an activity to be included in one school, yet omitted in another. In recent years physical education has accommodated a widening range of activities, and now with health topics it has to find space for yet more. The dilemma of the boundaries of physical education arises when topics such as sexuality, body abuse and nutrition are taught under the umbrella of physical education. These topics certainly pertain to the body, but they stray from the notion of physical activity itself.

Physical Education Teachers Are Not Health Educators

This kind of issue is also highlighted by Williams (1978) in her claim that physical education teachers are not, logically, teachers of health education. This comment is based upon the argument that each subject has certain criteria that give it its unique nature, like its aims, content and methods of teaching. Williams then argued that 'if there is such differentiation between subject areas, then a teacher of one subject cannot, conceptually speaking, be the teacher of another subject at one and the same time' (p. 116).

Teachers of health education will need to possess substantial levels of knowledge about health concepts and, by selection of relevant subject matter and teaching methods, assist the development of decision-making skills in children. Although this argument does serve to provide a warning that a health focus in physical education is not as straightforward as it may seem, it does appear to take an all-or-nothing stance. Certainly, it would be a formidable task for any person to become a genuine authority in, and specialist teacher for, both physical education and health. However, primary school teachers, in the main, are teaching children rather than subjects and have to cope with far more than just two elements of the curriculum. Williams's argument also overlooks the affinity between the two disciplines. This affinity has been illustrated by the Health and Physical Education Project (Dowling, 1986, p. 1), as shown in Figure 2.1. Although the figure has a number of omissions from the 'Health education' circle, such as obesity and stress management, whilst outdoor education and martial arts are missing from 'Physical education', the links between the two are clear; there would certainly seem to be potential for integration of subject matter.

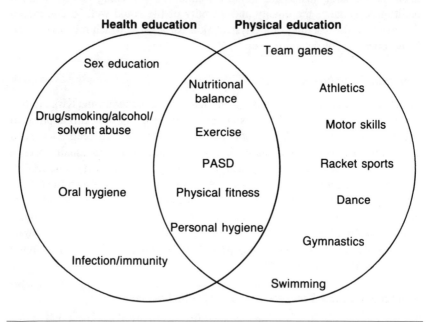

Figure 2.1   The relationship of health education to physical education. Reprinted by permission of Len Almond, Director of Health Education Authority Health and Physical Education Project, Loughborough University, Loughborough, Leicestershire.

Poor Justification for Health as an Objective of Physical Education

The resurgence of health as an objective for physical education has rekindled the old criticism that a justification for health is based only on its extrinsic value. This point revolves around the issue of whether health-related fitness is only valued insofar as it is a means to an end, particular forms of physical activity bringing about a state of fitness or health. This is undoubtedly often true, but the same could be said in the case of learning to swim to avoid drowning, in learning skills for competitive performances and even in experiencing physical activities as potential lifelong recreational pursuits. All such physical education experiences have an instrumental purpose.

However, the important factor is that the outcomes are dependent upon an individual valuing physical activity for its own sake. For example, the chances of an activity becoming a lifelong recreational pursuit must be greatly enhanced if the individual has a love of that particular activity. The chances of an individual maintaining an active lifestyle for the benefit of health are likewise much greater if the activity has intrinsic value:

> We want people to go jogging because they enjoy that act of jogging, . . . to swim because they enjoy the act of swimming. We want people to experience satisfaction and pleasure during the actual engagement in the activity and not just on its conclusion or afterwards through a sense of achievement or relief. (Hargreaves, 1981, p. 27)

Concluding Remarks About Reservations

Thus, in conclusion, it could be argued that the promotion of health is in fact a 'core' objective of physical education in schools. It offers a unique contribution that probably could not be offered as effectively elsewhere. It facilitates optimum physical growth and educates pupils about the many health attributes of lifelong physical activity. In fact, it is difficult to envisage how other objectives could be justified as strongly as health. Without good health, individuals could not easily play sport, engage in physical recreation or even gain aesthetic appreciation from athletic endeavour.

The Importance of Promoting Health in Primary School Physical Education

The Health and Physical Education Project has sparked immense interest in health-related fitness amongst secondary schools; this appears to be leading to widespread adoption of a health focus to physical education (Almond, 1988). Not so much attention has been paid to the primary age range; yet it is exactly in these early years that lifestyles are crystallizing.

Bray (1987) has highlighted three aspects of primary schools that facilitate the promotion of physical health principles. First, primary-age children are curious about their own bodies and particularly receptive to information about physical health. Second, because the classroom teacher oversees the all-round development of the child, it is possible to integrate various elements of healthy behaviour into a meaningful whole rather than isolating them into separate compartments, as often happens at secondary level. Third, there is very often a close liaison with the home, which can be a useful mechanism for influencing parents, something clearly important if genuine changes are to be effected.

There are four major reasons for justifying health as an objective in primary physical education. They are

- the contribution of physical education to sound growth and development,
- promotion of the value of habitual physical activity,
- the establishment of a physically active lifestyle, and
- prevention of cardiovascular disease risk factors.

The Contribution of Physical Education to Sound Growth and Development

Physical education has a long tradition of helping establish a sound physique in childhood, thus providing the basis for long-term health benefits. It was recognized by the ancient Greeks (Van Dalen & Bennett, 1971), revived in Renaissance Italy (McIntosh, Dixon, Munrow, & Willetts, 1973) and confirmed in the 1980s by the Fitness and Health Advisory Group to the Sports Council (Fitness and Health Advisory Group, 1988).

In fulfilling this role, physical education has sometimes been seen as a means of countering the effects of poor diet and inadequate living conditions. Although there have been improvements over the years, many of Britain's children still seem to suffer from these problems (Child Poverty Action Group, 1989). It is widely accepted that physical education fosters the sound development of bones, muscles and joints and contributes to health-related elements such as posture, hygiene and safety. Additionally, it is evident that obesity is a growing problem and that body fatness in adult life originates in early childhood (Garn & Lavelle, 1985). Surely few would deny that the primary years are a crucial period for growth and that there is thus a prominent role for a health focus to physical education at this time.

Promotion of the Value of Habitual Physical Activity

Undoubtedly, values are fashioned over many years, but it is clear from socialization theory (Kelly, 1977) that pervasive influences occur in childhood. The natural physical exuberance of young children can be stifled by modern living conditions, and negative dispositions to physical activity can often be traced back to negative experiences of physical activity in childhood (Wankel, 1988). A physical education curriculum that provides all children with pleasant and enjoyable experiences of physical activity can lead them to view physical activity as a positive and rewarding element of life, something valued rather than despised.

The Establishment of a Physically Active Lifestyle

It cannot be denied that adult lifestyles are resistant to change and that it is supremely difficult to turn a passive lifestyle into an active one. The evidence shows that adults (Health Promotion Trust, 1987) and adolescents (Armstrong, 1988) are relatively inactive and will not easily be persuaded to become more active (Dishman & Dunn, 1988). If young children can be motivated to engage in active lifestyles and powerful reasons are given for their maintenance throughout life, the reactivation process may not be needed in the end.

Prevention of Cardiovascular Disease Risk Factors

It has become clear that, in relation to coronary heart disease, the major risk factors of elevated serum cholesterol levels, cigarette smoking and hypertension emerge during youth and that the atherosclerotic process itself is present from infancy (Stary, 1983). Two other findings are particularly significant here. First, it is the case that atherosclerosis builds up with age, thus ever increasing the risk of cardiovascular disease for the individual (Berenson, Srinivasan, Freedman, Radhakrishnamurthy, & Dalferes, 1987). Second, data from the Bogalusa Heart Study in America 'demonstrate that the percentile rank a child holds for total serum cholesterol levels and beta-lipoprotein cholesterol at a young age tends to be maintained relative to his/her peers and tracks through adolescence into adulthood' (Wynder, 1988, p. 5). In other words, those children identified at an early age as most at risk tend to remain the ones most at risk as they get older. There is thus a strong case for early promotion of healthy behaviours to prevent the occurrence of heart disease risk factors as well as for early identification and subsequent follow-up screening of heart disease risk factors.

There is now little doubt that an active lifestyle can help protect an individual from heart disease (Powell, Thompson, Casperson, & Kendrick, 1987). Primary school physical education has a major role to play in this aspect of disease prevention.

Review of Initiatives Emphasizing Health as an Objective for Primary Physical Education

Until the 1980s, efforts to increase the physical activity levels of schoolchildren had mainly been aimed at improving levels of physical fitness. Improved fitness was then expected to enhance the general health of the individual child. The promotion of active lifestyles is now seen by many as instrumental in modifying heart disease risk factors. Consequently, most initiatives that have emphasized health as an objective for physical education have been predominantly concerned with the promotion of heart health. Two particular approaches discernible in primary education are shown in Table 2.1.

Table 2.1   Initiatives Aimed at Increasing Physical Activity Levels of Primary School Children

Integrated heart health programmes	Physical activity programmes in addition to normal curricula
Body Owner's Manual (Australia)	Vigorous Exercise Programme (USA)
Know Your Body (USA)	Trois Rivières Study (Canada)
Go for Health (USA)	Daily Physical Education (Australia)
Heart Smart (USA)	Total Concept of Physical Education (Scotland)

Integrated Heart Health Programmes

The Body Owner's Manual

Integrated heart health programmes aim to influence lifestyles by providing education about risk factors such as diet, smoking and physical activity. Worsley and Coonan (1984) reported the effects of a heart health education programme aimed at primary age children in Australia. This programme, based upon an imaginative pupil workbook called The Body Owner's Manual, provided information on the workings of the body and considered the relationship between lifestyle, health and disease. Four hundred twenty 10-year-old children were divided into the following four treatment groups, all of which received daily physical education:

- Control
- Performance targets and self-monitoring of performances
- Two heart health lessons per week for 6 months
- Two heart health lessons per week for 6 months plus performance targets and self-monitoring of performances

The results showed that children in the group with combined treatment of heart health education and self-monitoring, exhibited the greatest improvement in health knowledge and physical health status. Intriguing were findings that the group in which the children simply monitored their own performances improved more than the control group and that their gains in health knowledge were only slightly less than the combined treatment group. In this case, the process of self-monitoring generated an interest in health and perhaps stimulated discovery of health concepts. This early study did, however, indicate that there might be considerable value in relating classroom work to physical education lessons.

The Know Your Body Programme

In America there have been many attempts to provide comprehensive heart health programmes for primary school children. One example, supported by the American Health Foundation, is the Know Your Body programme, which was launched in New York in 1979 (Wynder, 1988). This programme initially involved over three thousand 9-year-old pupils who were randomly assigned to intervention or control groups. For approximately 2 hours per week, intervention groups experienced a health promotion curriculum that included content related to nutrition, physical fitness and cigarette smoking. Evaluation of the programme indicated positive results for the intervention groups in terms of a reduction in total cholesterol, an increase in heart health knowledge and a substantially lower initiation rate for cigarette smoking. There was, however, no effect on body mass, physical fitness or blood pressure (Walter, Hofman, Vaughan, & Wynder, 1988).

The current Know Your Body programme contains many interesting features. For example, there is an annual screening process consisting of a physical examination to identify risk factors amongst children. Any pupil considered to be 'at risk' is given an enhanced heart health programme to reduce the elevated risk. All children are given a 'health passport', which, amongst other things, enables them to record their cholesterol levels and encourages the individual child to take responsibility for the maintenance of his or her health.

The Go for Health Project

Based in Texas in the United States, the Go for Health project is another innovative attempt to reduce cardiovascular disease risk factors amongst primary school children. The administrators maintain that, in order to influence health-related behaviour, education alone is not sufficient:

> Classroom instruction can emphasize cognitive, affective and skill outcomes, but children cannot practice what they learn if offered only high-fat, high sodium foods and low intensity physical activities at school. The school environment should enable and reinforce healthful behaviour. (Parcel et al., 1987, p. 151)

The two main concerns of this health promotion project are dietary and physical activity practices. In addition, therefore, to heart health classroom instruction, Go for Health seeks to reduce fat and sodium in school meals and shift the emphasis of physical education towards aerobic fitness. Organizational change is effected by the formation of a task force in each primary school. The cafeteria manager, physical education teachers, classroom teachers, school nurses and PTA members organize school fun runs, health promotion activities, presentations at PTA meetings, food tasting and a Go for Health newsletter.

Quite an extreme position is taken for physical education: Aerobic activity is proposed as the main focus of the physical education curriculum. This approach was taken in response to low levels of aerobic activity evidenced in existing physical education lessons and in order to further the aim of improving cardiovascular fitness and fostering lifelong activity. Three instructional units for physical education were developed to be taught over a 6- to 8-week period. The three units are divided into

- running and aerobic calisthenics;
- aerobic obstacle course and aerobic dance; and
- aerobic circuit training, cross-country and jump rope.

Evaluations of the project are still awaited, but it will be interesting to see not only whether pupil effects are favourable but also how the schools and the teachers react to the kinds of organizational change described.

The Heart Smart Programme

Based in New Orleans, Louisiana, in America, the Heart Smart programme contains elements of the three initiatives previously described, yet adds a further imaginative dimension to the evaluation process (Downey et al., 1987). Thus, in common with the other projects, a classroom-based heart health education programme has been implemented, and efforts have been made to modify existing infraschool structures such as school lunch, school health services and extracurricular activities. The physical education curriculum is supplemented by a year-long 'Superkids-Superfit' exercise programme. In addition to an emphasis upon aerobic activities such as interval workouts and rope skipping, all lessons begin and end with 5 minutes of walking and static stretching. Children are encouraged to design personal exercise plans and are helped in this through the use of an individualized log book. Numerous schoolwide strategies are also employed, including an 'afternoon perk-up', where an exercise tape is broadcast over the school's public address system!

The main difference between this initiative and the other projects, however, relates to its experimental design and evaluation. The Heart Smart study involves a comparison of the effectiveness of 'population' and 'high-risk' approaches. In the population approach, attempts are made to improve the health-related behaviours of the total pupil population in a school. In the high-risk approach, children identified through screening as having a high risk of suffering from heart disease (albeit at some time in the future) experience an intensive family health promotion programme. This consists of weekly group-oriented activities for both children and parents, with subsequent monthly follow-up sessions.

The results, still awaited, will have important implications for future heart health programmes. Although potentially quite efficient, the high-risk strategy does rely on the supposition that young children identified as 'at risk' will in fact turn out to be the main sufferers of heart disease. Although the evidence appears to point in this direction, there would seem to be a need for subsequent general screening to identify late developers on risk factors.

Physical Activity Programmes in Addition to the Normal School Curricula

Most attempts to enhance long-term physical activity levels have been based upon theoretical principles that support the introduction of cognitive and affective components into the educational process. As a result, the individual is helped to understand why it is important to be active and is encouraged to develop a positive orientation to physical activity. There is also a school of thought holding that giving children additional, vigorous physical activity over and above normal physical education lessons will not only improve physical fitness, hence health status, but will establish a routine of habitual physical activity that would be instinctively continued in the long term. Four investigations carried out with primary-age children are now considered.

Vigorous Exercise Programme

In the United States MacConnie and co-workers examined whether the intensity of daily physical activity could be raised for 6- and 7-year-olds (MacConnie, Gilliam, Greenen, & Pels, 1982). Fifty-nine children were assessed according to height, weight, skinfold measurement and resting heart rate. A randomly selected experimental group was given an 8-month programme of 25 minutes of vigorous aerobic exercise four times a week. The experimental group also had a 20-minute heart health lesson once a week.

Whilst there were no significant differences in physical characteristics between the two groups, the physical activity patterns showed that 'the experimental group spent significantly more time than the control group at heart rates greater than 160 beats per minute' (p. 205). The vital question, however, is whether or not the additional sessions encouraged any voluntary activity over and above that required by the intervention. On this point the authors unequivocally stated that the total high-intensity activity figures could not be accounted for by pre-intervention levels and exercise sessions alone. Extra vigorous activity must have been initiated by the children themselves. MacConnie and associates concluded that this kind of programme could lead to the adoption of healthy habits but that longer term effects needed to be examined.

The Trois Rivières Study

Whilst the exercise programme just described seemed to have no influence upon the physical characteristics of 6- and 7-year-olds, the Trois Rivières study in Canada did record improvements in children aged 10 to 12 after additional physical activity (Shephard, Jequier, La Vallee, LaBarre, & Rajic, 1980). Over 500 boys and girls were given 5 hours of additional physical activity per week with an emphasis upon the development of cardiorespiratory and muscular endurance. They were compared with a control group who received only the standard 40-minute period of physical education each week. Using diary accounts and retrospective activity questionnaires, patterns of physical activity were assessed after the children had participated in the programme over a period of 4 to 5 years.

The results established total daily physical activity (light, moderate and vigorous) at 3.73 hours per day for the experimental group and 3.43 hours per day for the control group. Although there was actually less out-of-school physical activity recorded for the experimental group, the additional school physical activity more than made up for this. Compared with the MacConnie study (1982), the children were not stimulated to undertake extra, voluntary physical activity. Perhaps there is a saturation point, however, because the children in the Trois Rivières experiment were given 5 hours of additional activity per week whilst those in the MacConnie study received slightly less than 2 hours per week. The prime objective of the Trois Rivières experiment had been to improve the fitness level of the experimental group, and it was certainly the case that they turned out to be superior to the control group in aerobic power and muscular strength.

Daily Physical Education

An Australian study reported by Dwyer and associates (Dwyer, Coonan, Leitch, Hetzel, & Baghurst, 1983) produced similar improvements in fitness as a result of extra physical education over a 14-week period but also added a further dimension in respect of results related to academic performances. Five hundred 10-year-old primary school children were split into two intervention groups and one control group. The intervention groups received daily physical education lessons of 1-1/4 hours, whilst the control group received their usual three half-hour lessons per week. Pre- and postintervention tests included physical measurements, academic performance and classroom behaviour. Despite the relatively short period of intervention, significant falls in body fat and increases in physical work capacity were noted in the groups receiving daily physical education, although there were no significant differences in blood pressure or lipid levels. There were no differences in academic performance registered, but the daily physical education groups seemed to exhibit improved classroom behaviour. Thus, despite the extra time devoted to the daily physical education regime, there was no detrimental effect upon academic performance. Also on the positive side, there were distinct health gains in body fat reduction and increased physical work capacity. Subsequent investigations indicated that similar advantages could be gained from a longer term daily physical education programme.

Developing a Total Concept of Physical Education

Another experiment in daily physical education for primary school pupils has been conducted in the Strathclyde region of Scotland (Pollatschek, Renfrew, & Queen, 1986). In this case, the main stimulus was not fitness improvement but rather a desire to develop a physical education programme for primary schools that could form a satisfactory basis for secondary school physical education. Two major features underpinned the experiment. First, a working party constructed a suitable physical education programme for primary pupils, which, interestingly, was divided into the following four areas: active health, dance, games skills and gymnastics. Second, a system of team teaching was introduced whereby secondary physical education specialists worked alongside primary colleagues from corresponding feeder schools.

Over a period of a year, 500 children from 9 to 11 years old experienced a daily 40 minute physical education programme. Both the children involved in the experiment and a matched control group were pre- and posttested on anthropometry, motor fitness, reading comprehension, computation and attitude to school. Qualitative data were also collected from all individuals connected with the experiment.

The main findings established that those children experiencing daily physical education had motor fitness scores superior to those of the control group and showed more positive attitudes to school. Significantly, despite the loss in classroom teaching time, the daily physical education group maintained academic performance in line with the control group, thus corroborating the findings of Dwyer and associates (1983). Of equal importance were the reactions of the primary schools: The class teachers were found to be unanimously in favour of the scheme. For example, they felt more confident in their teaching of physical education and relied less upon televised lessons. There was also a general consensus about improvements in the self-esteem of pupils and a noticeable reduction of indiscipline.

This would therefore seem to offer an exceptionally useful model on which to build a successful approach to primary school physical education that, additionally, incorporates a prominent health focus in the programme. The positive feedback from class teachers would seem to have been an especially significant factor because it is the acknowledged limitations of primary school teachers that so often prove the stumbling block with physical education, no matter how impressive the initiative.

There are several problems that emerge, however. First, this experiment was limited to 9- to 11-year-olds; quite clearly, the whole experience needs to be initiated upon entry to school and continued throughout. The resource implications of this for the team-teaching element are serious, and probably insurmountable given normal conditions. Second, the whole area of fitness testing for young children is riddled with controversy (Armstrong, 1987). Despite the rigorous nature of testing in this experiment, there will be doubt cast over the quality and meaning of the findings, and until there is wider agreement on this issue, it is perhaps wiser to seek criteria other than fitness measures as indicators of success.

Concluding Remarks About the Importance of Health Promotion

It has to be said that firm conclusions cannot be drawn about the effects of these attempts to promote health amongst primary school children. Many of the initiatives are in their early stages, and little is known about long-term effects on physical activity levels. Nevertheless, this review has indicated that gains in health knowledge, short-term increases in activity levels, and improvements in attitudes to healthy practices can be achieved. This ought to encourage further consideration of how a health objective might be assimilated into primary school physical education.

The Happy Heart Project

The Happy Heart Project is based at the University of Hull and is funded by the Health Education Authority's Look After Your Heart campaign and the National Children's Play and Recreation Unit. Its main aim is the promotion of active lifestyles amongst children of primary school age.

Theoretical Basis for the Happy Heart Project

To explain the current initiatives of the Project, it is necessary to refer briefly to health education theory. Dooley and Kellett (1986) have claimed that 'so far, physical educators have had little to do with promoting active life-styles' (p. 50). This rather contentious statement implies that, although physical education lessons

have contained physical activity, it is not necessarily the case that health education has been taking place; it is more likely to have been a kind of conditioning
process. In fact, although exercise programmes are rather more sophisticated
nowadays, they are not far removed from drill forms, which were supposedly
rejected many years ago. To underline this, McNamee (1988) has hinted that drill
might be considered to have reemerged, albeit camouflaged as aerobic sessions.
Although there is a certain danger that this may happen in practice, it would clearly
not be the intention of those who ascribe to the inclusion of a health focus in
physical education.

In a similar vein, Williams (1978) has intimated that the inclusion of health-
related fitness activities in the physical education programme has been based upon
the claim that physical education lessons might achieve the level of activity that
would promote fitness. McIntosh (1988) also suggested that physical education
programmes, even with the 5 per cent time allocation within the National Curriculum, could have a significant effect upon cardiovascular efficiency. However,
both Williams and McIntosh acknowledged that a physical education programme
based upon such principles would have to jettison other objectives. Indeed, the
aim cannot be to achieve fitness within physical education lessons. The futility
of this approach is becoming more and more apparent (Parcel et al., 1987). The
goal is surely to lead the individual child to take responsibility for his or her own
lifestyle, with the hope that the lifestyle will eventually include sufficient physical activity for health.

To achieve this goal, conventional wisdom has involved a move towards
'propositional knowledge' (knowledge of health principles) and away from
'procedural knowledge' (knowledge of how to perform skills) (McNamee, 1988).
Essentially, this means providing the why to children instead of just the how.
It is a misconception to believe that one must exclude the other; physical education has perhaps been less effective because teachers have not explained why more
often. Adopting a health focus to physical education, teachers are not only able
to explain why one ought to be active for health but also show how to perform
activities that lead to good health. Many prominent physical educators (Corbin,
1987; Cureton, 1987; Hargreaves, 1981; McIntosh, 1988) have given strong
support to this approach, which has been neatly summed up by Dooley and Kellett
(1986):

> For really worthwhile experiences, which have lasting beneficial effects upon
> children, physical fitness programmes in schools must have cognitive and
> affective as well as psychomotor objectives. . . . The key to promoting active
> life-styles is in promoting understanding itself. (p. 50)

This statement not only recognizes the value of increasing the child's health knowledge but also alludes to the need for efforts in the affective domain.

Colquhoun and Kirk (1987), however, have gone as far as to suggest that no
amount of knowing why and how will make any difference; information alone
will not necessarily alter behaviour. They have insisted that the affective domain
should be acknowledged, and this supposition has often been reiterated by Biddle
(1981). Certainly, it is very easy to say that one ought to encourage a positive

attitude to physical activity on the part of youngsters. This has always been asserted, yet low activity levels attest to the failure of physical educators to do just this. Fox and Biddle (1988) have proposed that physical educators should pay greater attention to the perceptions of children about physical education programmes and ensure that 'by the time our students leave physical education, they perceive that a wealth of benefits are inherent in physical activity and that the efforts involved in taking part are well worthwhile' (p. 82).

The effectiveness of a health education programme is always difficult to evaluate because there is no certainty that changes in behaviour are necessarily attributable to the programme itself: Many other influences, like family, friends and media, are also at work. The apparent lack of impact of early efforts led not only to attempts to improve the programmes themselves but also to a shift in overall philosophy. There is a feeling now that, however good, education alone cannot be really effective. Thus, the concept of 'health promotion' has emerged, whereby a healthy environment becomes the ultimate aim (World Health Organization, 1986); such an aim has been a feature of some of the heart health programmes reviewed earlier in this chapter.

Putting Theory Into Practice With the Happy Heart Project

With regard to physical activities and the primary school child, there can obviously be many barriers to involvement (e.g., lack of encouragement from parents). The Happy Heart Project's version of health promotion therefore is to create what we call the 'active school', wherein every facet of school life facilitates and encourages rewarding physical activity. We encourage the headteacher and the staff to exhibit positive attitudes to physical activity for health, offer a range of imaginative resources and ensure that vital support is provided by parents and outside agencies.

A diagrammatic representation of the main features of the active school model is shown in Figure 2.2.

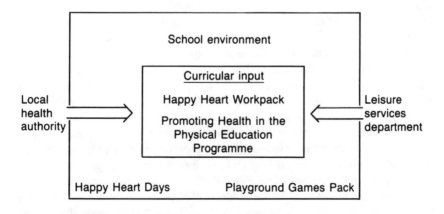

Figure 2.2 The active school.

Thus, we believe that the promotion of health in primary school physical education can be meaningful and effective only when offered as part of a total health promotion scheme. It would seem crucial to acknowledge that programmes in schools need to have cognitive and affective as well as physical objectives. This means that there has to be integration of practical work with classroom experiences because mere training or conditioning is unlikely to produce active lifestyles in the long term. This further seeks to overcome the problem mentioned by Bray (1987) that physical education in the primary school has been traditionally seen as recreational and mostly isolated from an otherwise integrated day.

In terms of the curriculum, we have produced a classroom workpack that aims to educate 5- through 11-year-olds about the relationship between physical activity and health. Although a greater knowledge of health principles in no way ensures logical or sensible behaviour, smoking being the typical example, it has to be a worthwhile starting point. Lack of knowledge can lead to prejudice and thoughtless behaviour. However, if an individual is armed with an understanding of certain basic facts and there is some influence upon values, attitudes and decision-making skills, there is potential for a healthy lifestyle to emerge. Hopefully, the workpack is soundly based, embracing the following educational principles that presently carry favour amongst many educationalists:

- Experiential approach to invoke personal involvement and meaning
- Learning by doing involving discovery, problem solving and practical activities
- Content aimed at developmental level of pupil
- Integration with other curriculum areas

During trials, there has been some indication of the workpack's effectiveness in enhancing short-term heart health knowledge.

The question then arises as to how physical education itself might promote health in the primary school setting. One way would be to suggest that during physical education lessons, every opportunity be taken to emphasize health points. The weakness of this approach is that in practice it will inevitably lack coordination and will always be in contention with other objectives. Even the most conscientious teachers might not cover all physical health issues, and it is unlikely that there would be any genuine progression through a child's primary school career.

A more sensible strategy would seem to be one where a half-term block of physical education lessons illustrate how physical activity can contribute to health. With this kind of emphasis, a powerful impact can be made and a new block of work can be undertaken each year to build upon the previous one. Similar health-related fitness programmes have been tried out in primary schools in other countries (Queensland Department of Education, 1987), yet they appear to have some serious shortcomings because their approach is mainly didactic, the content is dull, and they may mislead children into thinking that physical activity has to be painful to be beneficial. This could well have the opposite effect of what is intended in that it might put children off physical activity for life. In trying to avoid this situation, we have developed guidelines that promote physical activity for health in an exciting, pleasant and rewarding way and, where appropriate, encourage the children themselves to contribute ideas and devise activities.

In the extracurricular setting we are currently promoting other initiatives. For example, we have developed a Playground Games Pack, which encourages games involving vigorous activity. Such packs have been received with great enthusiasm by teachers and supervisory staff anxious to stimulate purposeful play and reduce antisocial behaviour. We are also suggesting that schools organize Happy Heart Days, where a whole day focuses on physical activity in some shape or form. Whether it be in assemblies, lessons, playtimes or mass events, the message that physical activity is important will percolate through to the children. Although Happy Heart Days are one-off occasions, it is always emphasized that opportunities for the continuation of physical activity should be illustrated. This is where another vital ingredient of the promotion package emerges.

In attempts to provide links between school and community, we invite bodies such as Local Health Authorities, Leisure Services Departments and Parent Teacher Associations to become involved in the process. To date they have responded very well, helping us fashion an environment where the primary school child has every opportunity to get active and stay active.

Final Comments

Many countries are now experimenting with the idea of health promotion in the primary school setting. As yet nobody knows how effective this kind of approach will be. For any widespread effect it is clear that success is dependent not just upon the promotion itself but the quality of dissemination and the maintenance of the promotion (Kolbe, 1986). In essence, this means that both initial and in-service training needs be met together with adequate resourcing of schools.

This chapter has illustrated how other countries have invested in research and development. In Britain we can learn from their experience and build an approach to suit our unique traditions and culture. It is our experience that primary school teachers are most receptive to the notion of developing an active school. In the midst of the turmoil caused by National Curriculum issues, standardized testing and grumbles about low pay, one normally inactive teacher was overheard to comment, 'To tell you the truth I'm really looking forward to this term. This is the most exciting project I've experienced in "x" years of teaching.'

References

Almond, L. (1988). Do children take enough exercise? In Coronary Prevention Group (Eds.), *Should the prevention of coronary heart disease begin in childhood?* (pp. 29-36). London: Coronary Prevention Group.

Armstrong, N. (1987). A critique of fitness testing. In S.J.H. Biddle (Ed.), *Foundations of health related fitness* (pp. 136-138). London: Ling.

Armstrong, N. (1988). Children's physical activity patterns and coronary heart disease. In Coronary Prevention Group (Eds.), *Should the prevention of coronary heart disease begin in childhood?* (pp. 37-44). London: Coronary Prevention Group.

Åstrand, P.-O. (1987). Setting the scene. In Coronary Prevention Group (Eds.), *Exercise heart health* (pp. 5-20). London: Coronary Prevention Group.

Bar-Or, O. (1987). A commentary to children and fitness: A public health perspective. *Research Quarterly for Exercise and Sport*, **58**, 304-307.

Berenson, G.S., Srinivasan, G.R., Freedman, D.S., Radhakrishnamurthy, B., & Dalferes, B.S., Jr. (1987). Review: Atherosclerosis and its evolution in childhood. *American Journal of Medical Science*, **294**, 429-440.

Biddle, S. (1981). The 'why' of health related fitness. *Bulletin of Physical Education*, **17**, 28-31.

Board of Education. (1905). *Syllabus for physical training in schools*. London: Her Majesty's Stationery Office.

Bray, S. (1987). Health and fitness in the primary school. In N. Armstrong (Ed.), *Health and fitness in the curriculum* (pp. 6-18). Exeter: University of Exeter.

Child Poverty Action Group. (1989). *Declaration for a fairer Britain*. London: Author.

Colquhoun, D., & Kirk, D. (1987). Investigating the problematic relationship between health and physical education: An Australian study. *Physical Education Review*, **10**, 100-109.

Corbin, C.B. (1987). Youth fitness, exercise and health: There is much to be done. *Research Quarterly for Exercise and Sport*, **58**, 308-314.

Cureton, K.J. (1987). Commentary on 'Children and fitness: A public health perspective'. *Research Quarterly for Exercise and Sport*, **58**, 315-320.

Dishman, R.K., & Dunn, A.L. (1988). Exercise adherence in children and youth: Implications for adulthood. In R.K. Dishman (Ed.), *Exercise adherence: Its impact on public health* (pp. 155-200). Champaign, IL: Human Kinetics.

Dooley, L.E., & Kellett, D.W. (1986). Health-related fitness: Its implications for the primary school P.E. curriculum. *Physical Education Review*, **9**, 49-52.

Dowling, F. (1986). *An overview of the project and the foundations for a rationale of a health focus in physical education* (Occasional paper produced by the Health Education Authority Health and Physical Education Project). Loughborough: Loughborough University.

Downey, A.M., Frank, G.C., Webber, L.S., Harsha, D.W., Virgilio, S.J., Franklin, F.A., & Berenson, G.S. (1987). Implementation of 'Heart Smart', a cardiovascular school health promotion program. *Journal of School Health*, **57**, 98-104.

Dwyer, T., Coonan, W.E., Leitch, D.R., Hetzel, B.S., & Baghurst, R.A. (1983). An investigation of the effects of daily physical activity on the health of primary school students in South Australia. *International Journal of Epidemiology*, **12**, 308-313.

Fitness and Health Advisory Group. (1988). *Children's exercise, health and fitness*. London: Sports Council.

Fox, K., & Biddle, S. (1988). Children's participation motives. *British Journal of Physical Education*, **19**, 79-82.

Garn, S.M., & Lavelle, M. (1985). Two decade follow-up of fatness in early childhood. *American Journal of Diseases of Children*, **139**, 181-185.

Hargreaves, A. (1981). The intrinsic value of exercise. *Bulletin of Physical Education*, **17**, 26-27.

Health Promotion Trust. (1987). *Health and lifestyle survey*. London: Author.

Kelly, J.R. (1977). Leisure socialisation: Replication and extension. *Journal of Leisure Research*, **9**, 121-132.

Kolbe, L.J. (1986, October/November). Increasing the impact of school health promotion programs: Emerging research perspectives. *Health Education*, pp. 47-52.

MacConnie, S.E., Gilliam, T.B., Greenen, D.L., & Pels, A.E. (1982). Daily physical activity patterns of prepubertal children involved in a vigorous exercise program. *International Journal of Sports Medicine*, **3**, 202-207.

McIntosh, P.C. (1972). *Physical education in England since 1800*. London: Bell.

McIntosh, P.C. (1988). *My favourite subject: A report on physical education and school sports for Inner London*. London: Inner London Education Authority.

McIntosh, P.C., & Charlton, V. (1985). *Impact of Sport for All policy: 1966-84*. London: Sports Council.

McIntosh, P.C., Dixon, J.G., Munrow, A.D., & Willetts, R.F. (1973). *Landmarks in the history of physical education*. London: Routledge.

McNamee, M. (1988). Health-related fitness and physical education. *British Journal of Physical Education*, **19**, 83-84.

Munrow, A.D. (1972). *Physical education: A discussion of principles*. London: Bell.

Parcel, G.S., Simons-Morton, B.G., O'Hara, N.M., Baranowski, T., Kolbe, L.J., & Bee, D.E. (1987). School promotion of healthful diet and exercise behaviour: An integration of organisational change and social learning theory interventions. *Journal of School Health*, **57**, 150-156.

Pollatschek, J., Renfrew, T., & Queen, J. (1986). The development of a total concept of physical education. In *Trends and developments in physical education: Proceedings of the VIII Commonwealth and International Conference on Sport, Physical Education, Dance, Recreation and Health* (pp. 57-60). London: E & F.M. Spon.

Powell, K.E., Spain, K.G., Christenson, G.M., & Mollenkamp, M.P. (1986). The status of the 1990 objectives for physical fitness and exercise. *Public Health Reports*, **101**, 15-21.

Powell, K.E., Thompson, P.D., Casperson, C.J., & Kendrick, J.S. (1987). Physical activity and the incidence of coronary heart disease. *Annual Review of Public Health*, **8**, 253-287.

Queensland Department of Education. (1987). *Physical education source book: Health related fitness*. Queensland, Australia: Author.

Shephard, R.J., Jequier, J., La Vallee, H., LaBarre, R., & Rajic, M. (1980). Habitual physical activity: Effects of sex, milieu, season and required activity. *Journal of Sports Medicine*, **20**, 55-66.

Stary, H.C. (1983). Structure and ultrastructure of the coronary artery intima in children and young adults up to age 29. In G. Schettler, A.M. Gotto, G. Middelhoff, A.J.R. Habenicht, & K.R. Jurutka (Eds.), *Atherosclerosis VI* (pp. 82-86). Berlin: Springer Verlag.

Van Dalen, D.B., & Bennett, B.L. (1971). *A world history of physical education*. Englewood Cliffs, NJ: Prentice Hall.

Walter, H.J., Hofman, A., Vaughan, R.D., & Wynder, E.L. (1988). Modification of risk factors for coronary heart disease. *New England Journal of Medicine*, **318**, 1093-1100.

Wankel, L.M. (1988). Exercise adherence and leisure activity: Patterns of involvement and interventions to facilitate regular activity. In R.K. Dishman (Ed.), *Exercise adherence: Its impact on public health* (pp. 369-396). Champaign, IL: Human Kinetics.

Williams, A. (1988, July/August). The historiography of health and fitness in physical education. *British Journal of Physical Education*, **19**(4/5) (Research Suppl. 3).

Williams, G. (1978). Physical education and health education: Necessary or contingent connection. *Physical Education Review*, **1**, 111-117.

World Health Organization. (1986). Health promotion: A discussion document on the concept and principles. *Public Health Review*, **14**(3/4), 245-254.

Worsley, A., & Coonan, W. (1984). Ten year olds' acquisition of body knowledge: The Body Owner's programme 1980, 1981. *Health Education Journal*, **42**, 114-120.

Wynder, E. (1988). Coronary heart disease prevention: Should it begin in childhood? In Coronary Prevention Group (Eds.), *Should the prevention of coronary heart disease begin in childhood?* (pp. 3-12). London: Coronary Prevention Group.

Yates, J. (1977). Ideology in physical education. *Bulletin of Physical Education*, **13**, 9-17.

Chapter 3

Physical Education and the National Curriculum

John Alderson
David Crutchley

The traditional curriculum pattern, established with the introduction of compulsory schooling in 1870, was directed at the promotion of literacy and numeracy, combined with elements of classical scholarship for the more able. Physical training was included to minimize the economic and military difficulties caused by an unhealthy and unfit populace. Once established, this initial curriculum pattern and all subsequent developments and innovations could not be seriously challenged by those outside the education system.

This model of the school curriculum was accepted by the majority of people because school was the major (if not the only) agency in young people's lives through which they could gain the information they needed to become educated. However, in recent years we have seen an information and communications explosion outside the education system. Children make considerable use of its sophisticated products: Cowie (1983) reports average television viewing rates of almost 25 hours per week for children age 5 through 15. Schools have not been able to keep up with technological developments, partly due to a lack of funding.

At the same time, technological developments have had, and continue to have, a profound effect upon people's working lives. Traditional skills are little needed; quite new skills are increasingly required. Above all, people need to be adaptable and are perceived as likely to have to change skills during their working lives, accepting retraining and updating as part of normal practice.

Despite the efforts of a minority of dedicated innovators, the traditional secondary curriculum programme has not kept pace with these developments. One might argue that the lack of scrutiny from outside the system and the lack of effective evaluation procedures within it have created a gap between the curriculum as recently offered and the need to prepare young people for life after school. Hewlett (1987) argues that the curriculum does not 'connect' with the demands of the world into which the school leaver is thrust. This view is increasingly held by students, their parents, employers and the government. The replacement of 'O' levels by the General Certificate of Secondary Education (GCSE) examination (with its less traditional assessment structure and greater emphasis on skill development), the steady introduction of the tertiary tier into education, the Education Reform Bill and the growing influence of the Training Agency all demonstrate the government's commitment to hasten the pace of change in education. This commitment is expressed as a desire to satisfy the 'end-user', whether that be at the level of the individual, industry or the state.

This, then, is why we are to have a National Curriculum: The government has decreed it on the grounds of developing greater relevance in schooling. Irrespective of political beliefs and fears of increased central control, the introduction of a National Curriculum does offer educationists a structured opportunity to re-examine the secondary/tertiary curriculum with a view to providing a relevant 'education for life' in the twenty-first century.

Issues Facing Physical Education in the Development of a National Curriculum Statement

Elizabeth Murdoch (1986) alluded to the rich and meaningful past of physical education before stating her concerns about its current instability and future difficulties. She cited a number of reasons for this state of affairs.

Lack of Conceptual Clarity

Murdoch expressed her concern, shared by others, that the profession has failed to express clearly what physical education is and 'what it is aiming and able to do' (p. 83). Parry (1988) suggests this is because there has been a 'virtual absence of PE from serious, detailed, informed and open discussion at national level' (p. 106).

In a superficial sense, 'everybody' knows that in physical education children engage in activities such as football, athletics and swimming. Some may also be aware of movement activity or health-related fitness. But what is it that children should *know* of, be able to *do* in, and *appreciate* about these activities in which they participate? There appears to be professional consensus neither as to what being 'physically educated' really means nor as to how that state is best achieved as far as curriculum content and teaching methodology are concerned. The profession currently lacks any systematic means of evaluating the effectiveness of its teaching. In short there is, in large measure, a simple belief that involving children in a selection of physical activities will achieve valuable educational ends.

We are all aware of schools in which the physical education programme is based on the presentation of a fairly narrow selection of often highly traditional activities rather than on any cogent decisions about what it is that the programme is trying to achieve for pupils. Most teaching is directed at helping students improve their skills in activities, but it is often difficult, through either discussion or observation, to discover any other direction or focus for the work. Experience over the past 20 years indicates that the physical education profession, at all levels, appears to have great difficulty in handling innovation. We have given insufficient time to experimenting with and evaluating new ideas. We seem habitually to react either by rejecting new ideas out of hand or by accepting them wholesale and without criticism, the latter reaction often being accompanied by the total rejection of notions or beliefs previously held dear.

It seems unlikely that such problems are attributable to a single cause. Some possible factors are

- the lack of a constructively critical perspective within teacher training, and hence within teaching itself;
- the fact that teachers have neither the time nor the skills to plan and evaluate their work effectively enough;
- the lack of an evaluative perspective and the discouragement of those who have doubts about or wish to question accepted practice;
- a preoccupation with sport competition and the development of talent;
- a suspicion that training institutions have admitted to the profession many people who are keenly interested in high-level sport but who are less interested in teaching or in the less able pupil; and
- fragmentation within the profession and a lack of unity amongst the various representative organizations.

Like the rest of the education profession, physical educationists have displayed a tendency towards reactionary thinking and an overreliance on tradition. We have noted with regret the apparent fall in interest within our subject, demonstrated in but one way by the very low levels of takeup of physical activity by school leavers. The profession has mounted several inquiries into the place and value of physical education in our schools (see the Appendix). They have resulted in a number of recommendations, largely in support of fairly traditional views of physical education in the schools. But what the profession has not done is to reappraise fundamentally our concept of physical education in the light of massive societal change. In speaking about the place of sport in the physical education curriculum, Parry (1988) put it like this:

To consider the place of sport on the PE curriculum means not only to ask descriptive questions about what is currently the case . . . but also to ask for reasons why sport *ought* to have a place. . . . This sort of questioning is conspicuous by its absence from many PE and sport documents and I believe it to be a very serious weakness which has contributed significantly to present day difficulties. (Parry, 1988, p. 106)

The National Curriculum debate offers the physical education profession the opportunity to undertake that reappraisal, to make coherent statements about the nature of the subject and its concept of the physically educated person who should emerge from the curriculum at 16+.

Inability to Identify Stages of Progression

Murdoch (1986, p. 83) bemoaned the lack of a 'shared corporate conviction in our rationale at different stages of the learning process'. Secondary physical education curricula rarely demonstrate obvious and logical progression. This is partly because, as we have just seen, the end point, the notion of the physically educated person, is but vaguely defined, and partly because we tend to teach activities in which expert performance lies well above the capabilities of the majority of our pupils. We may know very well what skills we expect of a county-level badminton player because there are reference points outside school in the world of competition. But what do or should we expect of a pupil at the end of a badminton unit in the 2nd-year core curriculum, or within a GCSE course, or as a 5th-year recreation option? What progression of skills, knowledge and appreciation should we expect within a particular activity, given that blocks of work are presented on more than one occasion during the individual child's total physical education programme?

Traditionally, the physical education profession has rejected the notion of fixed performance expectations at given ages, arguing that children have different abilities and develop at different rates. However, physical education is no different from any other subject in this respect. Whilst acknowledging the effect of individual difference variables, surely we should have an idea of what average levels of performance, knowledge, understanding of issues and so on we should be working towards in particular elements of the curriculum. We should also have in place the evaluation procedures that would allow the teacher to assess the progress of individual pupils towards, or even beyond, such course objectives. On a more pragmatic note, the Education Reform Bill's proposed assessment stages at 7, 11, 14 and 16 will require us to define stages of progression if our subject is to be accepted within the foundation curriculum. Once in place, these evaluation procedures will allow questions to be asked about the quality of the physical education programme itself and of its delivery, professional issues that are rarely addressed in any systematic way today.

The National Curriculum debate offers physical education the opportunity to define what stages of progression are required in order to produce the physically educated 16+ student.

An Unwillingness to Investigate the Roots of the Subject

Murdoch (1986) suggested that some physical education teachers are perhaps not always sufficiently willing to question the evolution of their subject both in terms of appropriate content and teaching methodology:

> This stems from a strongly held conviction that Physical Education is a practical subject and it is through the doing that most is achieved. This tends to beg the question of the role of the teacher firstly as an educator responding to changing needs and demands of young people in society, and reinforces

a traditional approach since if the changes are made in tune with changes in the individual activities over time then the programme is seen as updated and relevant. (p. 84)

Challenges to the Traditional Interpretation of Physical Education

This traditional interpretation may be questioned on three counts. First, there is a need to justify why the curriculum should contain such activities at all and, if so, which ones? This point is addressed in the upcoming section about the rationale for physical education in the national curriculum.

Second, the traditional interpretation supposes that the teaching of certain activities, notably games, should be guided by the rule structures of governing bodies. That is, the curriculum should be controlled by sport forms that have evolved to challenge the most skilful performers in the world, despite the fact that by definition the school population is not (and by far the majority never will be) capable of anything like that level of performance. Whilst rule modifications need to be noted and implemented, meaningful curriculum development in activity terms surely lies in the definition of appropriate stages in the learning process, as previously referred to. The profession needs to investigate more deeply the basic chemistry of differing activity types in order to design progressive teaching programmes that accommodate the needs of pupils as they grow older and more able. This notion is a far cry from the more simplistic adoption of 'mini' forms of the major activities, however valuable these may be at a specific point in the progress of a given pupil.

Third, the traditional approach embodies the belief that children develop personally and socially solely as a result of engagement in activities. For example, one justification for involving children in sport, and again notably in games, is that their experience with rules gives them a sense of fair play, one that may even transfer to life situations outside sport. The traditional view is that this 'morality' develops within pupils as a direct result of the specific rule decisions and general ethos of the sports in which they participate, presumably through some form of osmosis.

This assumption is untenable; again, there is no evidence to support it. Indeed, as Parry (1988, p. 109) questions, 'who would claim the McEnroes and Bests to be amongst the moral giants of our time?' despite the fact that they must have spent many more hours playing sport than the average member of the public and hence should have absorbed more morality. If physical education does want to influence attitudes about morality, and particularly about morality in sport, then the appropriateness of the practical teaching situation must be questioned. The games field or athletics track is surely not the best venue, nor the activity per se the best context, for a pupil to debate and appreciate morality as a concept, the significance of a professional foul or the implications of drug abuse. These are conceptual, not performance, issues, ones that impinge on students via the media on a regular basis and surely qualify for the professional attention of the educator in schools.

Physical Education as Preparation for Life

The example of morality raises the whole question of the role of physical education in preparing the pupil to be a consumer of sport during adult life. The communications revolution means that people of school age, as well as throughout the rest of their lives, are potentially exposed to sport and other physical recreation activities through television, the papers and specialist magazines. That same technological revolution is offering the population as a whole (though not all subgroups within it) more leisure time, more disposable income and a greater range of leisure opportunities than ever before.

These references to education for leisure raise issues concerned with what constitutes a proper leisure or recreation focus within physical education. It could be argued that physical educationists have tended to blur the distinction between education for leisure and the provision of recreational opportunity. The provision of the latter is a relatively simple process: The teacher sets up a programme of activities designed to generate short-term satisfaction for the participants. The danger lies in the perception that professional responsibility is met by merely providing fun through activity sessions. Whilst this might be sufficient justification for extracurricular time, it is difficult to justify as the purpose of the core programme.

Education for leisure, on the other hand, is more complex, requiring the development of certain levels of performance capability together with social and personal skills appropriate to given recreational contexts. This constitutes the base for the level of personal autonomy required for the individual pupil to make informed choices about recreation involvement within the extracurricular programme, outside school and during the many years when school is left far behind. We would argue that this interpretation of education for leisure provides a proper focus for the later stages of the physical education programme, with the objective of continued personal growth. Seen in this light, education for leisure has considerable implications for resource utilization and teaching methodology.

The national curriculum debate gives the physical education profession the opportunity to reassess its objectives in terms of the wide variety of sport consumer roles now available and to consider the range of teaching methods appropriate to the realization of those objectives.

Other Issues

These, then, are some of the factors that, in Murdoch's view, have produced a state of instability within the profession today. In 1986 she felt the situation was in need of urgent rectification:

> I have felt for some time now that time was running out for Physical Education. It either has to declare itself with as coherent a voice as possible that it knows where it is going, or it will disappear. (p. 85)

Parry (1988) has also remarked on the 'possible threat to the continued existence of (parts of) PE on the school curriculum' (p. 106). We are all aware of pressure on schools in general and on physical education in particular. Revenue budgets are low, school playing fields are being sold off, teacher conditions of service have militated against the extracurricular programme, there is little money for in-service training, and there is a degree of disinterest in the subject in older pupils, manifested as a decline in extracurricular involvement.

The School Sport Forum document (1988) recommends the following:

> The Secretary of State for Education, through the National Curriculum Council should recognise the unique importance of physical education in schools by requiring that a minimum of 10% of total curriculum time is devoted to it throughout the statutory years 5-16. (p. 7)

However much one might agree with this sentiment, there is little by way of *evidence* to support the claim. Physical education does not have the criterion of examination pass rates, or a perceived relevance to the economy, that some other subjects can boast. The figures for school leavers' continued participation in physical recreation are disappointing, to say the least! In the current climate of educational effectiveness, there is a great danger that a recommendation like this will be perceived as empty gesturing, *unless* it is supported by a clear and unequivocal rationale for physical education.

Perhaps this is the most obvious argument of all for a National Curriculum debate within physical education; surely one can get no nearer to the bottom line than the very survival of the subject in schools. What is crucially important is that the physical education profession sees the need for this reappraisal of its work and enters the exercise with a will. If the implementation of a National Curriculum is simply perceived as a threat to the more traditional view of the work, then it is inevitable that Murdoch's and Parry's fears for the future will be well founded.

The National Curriculum debate offers the opportunity to develop a curriculum model for physical education that teachers across the country can implement, evaluate and discuss. The results of this process, appropriately shared, should form the basis of continuous reappraisal. This view recognizes that in planning the National Curriculum for physical education, we are unlikely to get it 'all right first time'.

A Rationale for Physical Education in the National Curriculum

Physical education is part of a wider process of education. It follows that a rationale for physical education must relate in some meaningful way to the education process as a whole. It is generally agreed that education is a process that seeks to transmit, evaluate and enrich aspects of culture (see, for example, Bruner, 1972, and

Stenhouse, 1967). Its purpose is to assist people in developing their potential in order to enrich both their own lives and the culture to which they belong. This view of education implies a process which aims to

- introduce people to valued cultural forms,
- allow people to develop their talents with a view to their productive future use,
- foster knowledge and understanding,
- foster creativity,
- foster critical and evaluative perspectives,
- promote independence,
- promote sensitivity and concern for other people,
- assist people to develop social skills, and
- help people understand themselves and develop self-esteem.

Aims of Physical Education

The broad aims just listed differ quite markedly in type. The first aim refers to valued cultural forms, that is, to those fields of human involvement that corporately make up culture. Art, science, commerce, engineering and education itself might all be seen as valued cultural forms. The other aims in the list refer to latent abilities or capacities within individuals that need development in order to permit access to and engagement in valued cultural forms.

We are therefore forced to agree with Parry (1988, p. 117) that the place of physical education on the curriculum is dependent upon whether or not the activities it promotes are valued cultural forms. If this were not so, then claims about the development of social and personal competencies gained through physical education could not be justified, for there is not one of the personal and social objectives of physical education that could not be addressed by other means. For example, the use of team games in the physical education programme is often justified on the grounds that it develops co-operation. However, opportunities abound within the school curriculum for promoting co-operation through interactive group work that will meet with at least as much success as games sessions— and do so more cheaply!

Sport as a Valued Cultural Form

What then are the valued cultural forms that justify the presence of physical education in the curriculum? The most obvious is sport. Its value in our culture is demonstrated in the 1986 quotation from Nicholas Ridley, Secretary of State for the Environment, which forms paragraph C1 of the School Sport Forum document (1988):

> Sport plays a vital role in everyday life. We recognise its importance to people in the national and international scene. At home, sporting activity provides a healthy and enjoyable leisure pursuit; sport promotes civic and national

pride; it can assist social and community aims; it has a significant impact on the economy. Internationally, sport can extend British influence and prestige and promote trade and stability. (p. 5)

And we know, too, that sport is similarly valued all over the world. At local, national and international levels, sport is a 'commodity' with which people identify and through which shared experiences are generated. It is particularly interesting to note how quickly Third World nations begin to use sport as a symbol of their emerging status.

Though there is little doubt as to the importance of sport, it is a concept that has proved exceedingly difficult to define. Brackenridge and Alderson (1982) refer to sport as 'organised competitive activity' in which participants strive for 'ascendency' within an agreed, though arbitrary, rule framework. Whilst this definition serves for those activities that have competition as their central feature, the Sports Council certainly does not accept such a restrictive view of sport, seeking rather to promote all forms of physical recreation. The School Sport Forum document (1988, p. 5) supports this wider view of sport, adopting the four categories offered by the Council of Europe's 1976 'Sport for All' Charter.

Typology of Sport

We feel there are illogicalities within that particular typology and therefore present a modification of it, retaining the idea of four categories of sport.

Organized Competitive Activities. These are the activities that fit Brackenridge and Alderson's definition; they are universally accepted as sports. The competition fundamental to these sports can be enjoyed on different levels, ranging from fun games to international contests. However, the essence of all these activities, at whatever level they are played, is the contract that the participants enter into with one another to try to win. As far as competitive sport is concerned, it matters not who wins; what matters is that the participants are pitting their skills against those of others in whatever way the rules of the sport both demand and allow.

Because there are so many activities that belong to this category of sport, we feel it is relevant to subdivide it for the purpose of planning the physical education programme. We would offer the following major subcategories of gymnastic, athletic and game sports:

- *Gymnastic Sports*. In these activities the winners are those whose movements are deemed the best in qualitative terms, as assessed against a predetermined set of criteria (e.g. the BAGA code of points). This group includes artistic gymnastics, trampolining and figure skating. It also includes the sport forms of dancing, such as ice dance and ballroom dancing.

- *Athletic Sports*. In this group the judging procedures seek to determine which performance is fastest, longest, highest or strongest (conforming to the Olympic motto of 'citius, altius, fortius'). The group includes track and field athletics, cycle racing, ski racing, rowing and weight-lifting. A focus for this group is the participants' production of power, in both explosive and endurance forms.

• *Game Sports*. Scoring procedures in this category determine which player or team achieves territorial domination through goals, runs, touchdowns, target points, and so on. There are several different types of games; the following sub-division may help to identify family groups:

○ *Field Games*. The field is divided into equal halves; participants invade the opponents' territory, and controlled physical contact is permitted. The rules of these activities seek to minimize the incidence of injury through contact. Teams vie to control possession of the ball and create scoring chances. This group includes activities like hockey, football and lacrosse.

○ *Court Games*. The court is divided into equal halves; participants again invade the opponents' territory, but direct physical contact is not permitted. Teams vie to control possession of the ball and create scoring chances. Netball and basketball are the main examples of this group.

○ *Net Games*. The court is divided into equal halves by a net; participants attack the opponents' territory symbolically with the ball whilst remaining within their own ground. Play is reciprocal, players attempting to set up positional advantage in order to play a clear winning shot or force an error from opponents. This group includes tennis, badminton and volleyball. Squash is a special case in that there is only one 'half' of the court; opponents take it in turns to use that space to attack each other.

○ *Innings Games*. The territory is divided unequally into a striking area for the attacking team and a larger area into which the ball is struck that is defended by the fielding team. Only the striking team can score runs or points; the fielding side attempts to take the 'lives' of the striking side. Teams take it in turns to strike and field through innings. Examples of innings games include rounders, cricket and softball.

○ *Fighting Games*. In this group the territory to be attacked consists of the opponents themselves; participants vie to hit or hold opponents whilst having to defend themselves from reciprocal attack. In the main these activities derive from earlier forms of fighting in which serious physical damage was done. The rules of the modern activity forms define target areas and 'falls' in order to judge the winner. Rule structures also seek to minimize any physical damage to participants whilst rewarding skilful performance. The group includes boxing, judo and fencing.

○ *Target Games*. In this group participants score by successfully finding targets. The emphasis lies in skilful control, which is judged in terms of accuracy. Shooting, archery and darts are the members of this group that most obviously derive from military skills, whilst golf does not. In all these target sports, participants are not allowed to interfere with their opponents' performance. Billiards and snooker, by contrast, are target sports in which participants can attempt to control their opponents' play whilst scoring themselves.

Conditioning Activities.   These activities are designed to promote physical power, endurance and mobility, and/or mental discipline. Aerobics, circuit training, weight training, jogging, aspects of yoga and the noncompetitive aspects of the martial arts fall into this category. These activities are not by nature competitive in the sense that one participant seeks to beat another. Some of these activities, such as circuit training, arose originally from competitive sportspeople's efforts to prepare themselves physically for involvement in other activities. Some have been borrowed from cultures in which sport as defined in the West is unknown, such as yoga and karate. Others, like aerobics, have been developed specifically for a general health purpose.

As with competitive sport, these activities can be enjoyed over a range of levels. At one end of the continuum is light exercise, with minimal conditioning benefit; at the other, participants set the most extreme targets for physical efficiency in terms of strength, endurance capacity, flexibility or bodily form. In some cases, a competitive sport form has been derived from or relates to a conditioning activity, as with competitive weight-lifting and body-building.

Adventure Activities.   These activities are essentially concerned with overcoming natural obstacles and journeying over wild terrain. Traditionally, camping, mountaineering, rock climbing, canoeing, caving, sailing and skiing have fallen into this category. However, new forms emerge as a result of technological developments, so sand-yachting, river-rafting, windsurfing, all-terrain cycling, hang-gliding and green lane motor-cycling should perhaps be included in the list. Such activities are capable of providing the most testing challenge of the skills and endurance of participants. There are no rule structures or 'winners' as such. As with the previous categories of sport, there is a continuum of potential involvement in adventure activities, ranging from a casual paddle along the canal in a canoe to a Himalayan mountain expedition or a single-handed ocean voyage.

As well as tackling natural obstacles, the participant may face added difficulties from the weather. This combination has persuaded some to characterize adventure activities as those associated with risk to life and limb. Clearly there will always be a degree of risk associated with such activities, but it is not their essential characteristic. Indeed, it is a mark of the rock-climber's or caver's skill that in addition to rock or pot-holing technique, they can read weather conditions and utilize safety procedures effectively.

Like conditioning activities, adventure activities have been developed into competitive sport forms: White-water slalom, downhill skiing, dinghy sailing and speed climbing are all forms of competitive racing with rule structures and scoring systems. They are designed to produce winners as well as, or even at the cost of, the original adventure experience of travelling through rough terrain; hence they no longer belong in the adventure category per se.

New Games.   This group contains activities that have a point or purpose and a form of rule structure designed to promote co-operative rather than competitive experience. Examples of this group include Earthball, Boffing Sticks and Skinning the Snake.

Purpose of the Typology.   This typology is intended to show the breadth and variety of activities that might be collectively defined as 'sport'. We feel that they would all be acceptable to the Council of Europe and to our own Sports Council. We would suggest, too, that the typology helps illustrate that sport is a cultural form with which physical education is and should continue to be associated. We must next debate whether there are other cultural forms with which physical education should be associated.

Dance as a Valued Cultural Form

The one area of activity with which our typology of sport did not deal is dance. It is important to distinguish here between dance as art and dancing as a sport form. The distinction between art and sport should surely be made on the criterion of the point or purpose of the activity.

Ice dance, as seen at the world championships, is by definition a sport. The competitors' dancing is assessed by a panel of judges against a set of agreed criteria to see whose performance is the best; the same can be said for a ballroom dancing competition or the Scottish country dancing so popular at a Highland Games. When Torvill and Dean perform the same world-championship routine within the context of their ice dance show, however, they are no longer involved in sport. The spectators pay to see dance on ice; they see an ice ballet with its own particular artistic message, not a 4-minute routine designed to meet the particular structural requirements of a competition. Nobody awards marks; the audience simply appreciates the artifact. The same applies with either a classical or a modern ballet performance; the dancers display their art and no one would think of giving them marks for either their technical merit or their artistic impression, despite the fact that in both these senses breathtaking skill may be displayed.

We earlier referred to the observation that conditioning and adventure activities have both spawned competition sport forms. By contrast, John Curry began a process, which Robin Cousins and Torvill and Dean have continued, of developing an art form out of the competitive sports of figure skating and ice dance. The fact that *some* ice dancers are able to cross the boundary between sport and art, and that both dance and the gymnastic category of sport depend upon a qualitative appreciation of the form of movements, does not necessarily mean that they should be lumped together for educational purposes under the label of physical education.

Physical education's past concern for children's dance development is illustrated by the invention of its own art form, modern educational dance. It has to be said that the initiative in large measure failed. The activity was not particularly attractive to pupils, perhaps because it did not relate in their experience to more acceptable dance forms or perhaps because it was not sufficiently effective in sensitizing pupils to art through movement.

Students and teachers of physical education are generally reluctant to teach dance, which is perhaps the activity allocated the least curriculum time. Could this be because the cultural form of sport with which the majority of physical education teachers are so deeply involved is radically different from that of art? We have seen the emergence of *some* very good centres of dance in schools across the country, almost always, and quite acceptably, separate from the sport elements of the schools' programmes. They have taken 'dance as art' as their ethos. In short, those who have found real success in teaching dance to children have done so by relating to the associated art forms, like drama, mime and music. This observation again highlights the inescapable divide between art and sport as forms of culture. We must ask whether or not the people who are drawn to sport and who will promote sport effectively as teachers can be expected also to be enthusiastic about dance, and vice versa.

At this point, the reader might well conclude that we belong to that well-established group of dance-bashers. This is not the case; in fact, the reverse is true. Our point would be that since dance is clearly a valued cultural form, it should be part of the education process in the same way music and drama are. The difficulty lies in knowing how and where it should be located. Our own view, based on the preceding observations, is that physical educators have not proved to be the best people to promote dance and that it should be taught within departments of performing arts. We would reject the argument that if physical education teachers don't do it, it will die altogether. Rather, the evidence suggests that in the hands of sport-minded physical educators, its death as an art form is ensured. Having said that, there may be a legitimate place for dancing in physical education either (a) for young children during the development of those movement competencies that underpin involvement in the sport and art forms that require skilful action or (b) in those dancing competitions that are sports in their own right.

Health and Physical Education

During the last decade we have seen a surge of professional activity associated with health-related fitness. In a nutshell, pupils are being encouraged in a variety of ways to adopt lifestyles that include regular exercise and to develop positive attitudes in this respect for their long-term futures. Our view of education takes as its focus the development of the individual and the provision of opportunities for life enrichment. Health, as a theme, relates to this view of education because it implies much more than a rather simplistic notion of disease avoidance and the maintenance of cardiovascular fitness. Total well-being, including psychological health and stress management, is an integral part of the health theme.

It is widely recognized that a broadly defined health theme does not centre upon any one area of the curriculum; rather, it is a cross-curricular matter within which physical education has a part to play. Physical education should make its contribution in helping young people understand about attainment and maintenance of fitness and in introducing young people to activities through which physical and psychological health can be maintained. We suggest, therefore, that it would be inappropriate to look at health as a cultural form on a par with sport or art. The conditioning activities category of sport offers the natural home for physical education's contribution to the cross-curricular health theme.

The Notion of Sport Consumership*

The traditional approach to teaching physical education quite rightly emphasizes the participation role of the sport consumer, for example the games player, the gymnast or the canoeist. However, there are a number of other consumer roles within the culture of sport that school physical education has largely ignored. These include a person's involvement as an official (referee or scorer), a leader or coach, a spectator (live or canned) and a 'student' of a particular sport activity. The coaching award schemes of the national governing bodies, the educational programme of the National Coaching Foundation, the evolution of the Central Council for Physical Recreation's (CCPR) Sports Leadership Award and implementation of community sports development programmes all point to the importance of alternative sport-consumer roles both to facilitate provision of the playing experience for those who want it *and* as valuable recreational experience in its own right.

Both core and extracurricular physical education can and should offer structured opportunities for individuals to adopt more than one sport-consumer role. What is crucially important is that pupils be deliberately introduced to different consumer roles and to their potential value to the individual *and*, on the basis of that structured experience, that they be required to debate and assess that value in the context of their own recreation.

The Media's Role in Sport Consumption

An analysis of the TV and radio schedules, of the four or more back pages of both local and national papers, and of the contents of the ever-increasing number of specialist sports magazines gives ample evidence of media consumption by people whose interest and sport information requirements are much more catholic and sophisticated than simple matters of checking the home side's league position or the starting price on the afternoon's choice for the 3.30 at Newmarket. The consumers' interests include matters such as team selection, performance, evolution of tactics, player statistics, methods of training, diet, injuries and their treatment, coping with competitive pressure and evaluation of new equipment.

---

*This and subsequent sections are presented with acknowledgements to John Alderson (1985), "Scholarship in physical education: Implications for the curriculum." In *Proceedings of the 28th ICHPER World Congress* (pp. 38-43). London: Physical Education Association.

These aspects of the 'student's' or 'hobbyist's' involvement with sport are essentially cognitive. They may parallel or even replace the participation role; that is the individual's choice. Sport exists to be consumed in whatever ways the public finds attractive and satisfying within society's wider mores of acceptable taste.

Physical Education's Role in Sport Consumption

Over the years physical education has tended to infer that these other consumer roles are in some sense less important than that of the active participant or that the individual is unlikely to adopt other consumer roles in addition to participation. The traditional view is still that coaching and refereeing are activities to which a player turns as a consolation prize only when 'over the hill'. Surely this is a ridiculous philosophy; coaches and match officials are performers in their own right who must be exceedingly knowledgeable about the activity and develop a repertoire of specialist skills.

While playing a game may be an important, and in some cases necessary, prerequisite for the development of such skills, the idea that playing is necessarily preferable to refereeing, or that the responsibility of refereeing should not be shouldered before the onset of middle age, is surely preposterous! We are all aware that dissent and even verbal abuse of umpires is on the increase and that children are exposed to such behaviour regularly through the media. Hence, it would seem important that the physical education programme in schools should give pupils of all ages experience of match control at appropriate levels of complexity, followed by opportunities to discuss and draw conclusions about that consumer role. Such discussions should include reference to the concepts of rule-bound behaviour, morality in sport and the problems associated with rule abuse and should be set in the context of children designing and adapting activity forms.

Similarly, there is a strong argument that the skills of watching, analysing and shaping performance that are crucial to a potential future coaching role should be introduced at a relatively early age. This can easily be done within the physical education programme; indeed, it is intrinsic to those teaching styles that involve pupils actively in cognitive judgements about the performance of their peers.

If the programme in schools is to do justice to the individual pupil's needs as advocated in recent 'education for leisure' and 'health-related fitness' initiatives, then it must sensitize pupils to the full range of consumer possibilities and do so in a way that potentiates intelligent decision making. This constitutes an important element of educating pupils in the richness of sport as part of our culture. As such, it requires quite deliberate thought about curriculum content and the best methods of presenting it.

Understanding the Activities That Form Our Sport Culture

In Britain successive reports from Wolfenden (1960) to Yates (1984) have pointed to the need for more resources to allow people greater access to physical recreation. However, there has been parallel evidence to suggest that the facilities that are provided are not always taken up, especially by the school leaver. While it is true that there must be many other attractions for the school leaver at this important time of change in his or her life, we wonder whether at the end of at least 5 years of exposure to secondary physical education, pupils really do understand the potential of sport activity for generating personal satisfaction.

In most physical education programmes pupils are introduced to a variety of activities, each pursued in a designated block of time. In almost all cases, each activity is thus treated in isolation; very rarely are students asked to contrast and compare their *experience* of different activities, surely a necessary prerequisite of later decision making about recreational involvement. In the later stages of the physical education programme, they may well be offered 'options', but again we would ask on what basis is it expected that choices should be made? Recent comment, particularly from the United States, suggests that such choices have more to do with teacher personalities and obligatory postexercise showers than with any criteria related to the nature of the activities on offer.

Most programmes claim to give the student balance in the curriculum. This usually means, for example, that the pupils are taught some games, some gymnastic-type work, some athletics and so on. However, how often are children asked to *think about* these different categories of activity? Perhaps when they leave school, all children should be consciously aware of the different experiences generated, for example by the territorial contest of games, the energy-testing quality of athletic activities and the movement-copying demand of gymnastics, trampolining and the like. What is more, individuals should be able to relate their experiences in different activities to their own abilities and to the sense of satisfaction they personally derive from participation.

Because most of our teaching is done in a sports hall, on a playing field or in a pool, we have tended to favour the technical aspect of participation. All children learn a forward roll, a forehand drive and a sprint start. However, one could well argue for a different approach. The nature of sport is that of solving an arbitrary problem or meeting an arbitrarily defined target or challenge. For example, in soccer the aim is to score more goals than the opposition. The problem is encapsulated in the rule structure of the game, as is the behaviour that players may (and may not) adopt in trying to win. To play at all well one must not only know the *rule structure* but also understand the *tactical options* that derive from it. A player then makes tactical decisions in the game, which in turn require *technical skills* with the ball.

We would therefore argue that teaching should be based on an appropriate mix of rule structures, tactical possibilities and technical movement requirements. What seems certain is that pupils should be aware of these three levels of analysis of an activity and be able to relate them one to another. Indeed, this is the essence of the recent initiatives in 'teaching through understanding'. An added advantage of this approach is that our teaching can accommodate all the consumer roles mentioned earlier and do so at least from the beginning of secondary education.

In addition to these tactical and technical requirements, to say that activities also place physical demands on the participant—particularly regarding strength, mobility and cardiovascular fitness—is stating the obvious. Most if not all pupils have at least some awareness of what these terms mean. However, this awareness may well be associated with the rather unpleasant experiences of doing too much too soon, arising perhaps from a brief introduction to circuit training, the not-very-regular cross-country run or the over-zealous first pop-mobility session.

Surely it is important that pupils are taught the physical demands of activities in just the same way as they are introduced to the technical demands. And surely it is also important for them to appreciate that different activities and different levels of involvement make different physical demands. From this base, pupils would find out more about how their bodies work and could be led to appreciate that very important distinction between, for example, getting specifically fit for a given competitive sport and using a conditioning activity to promote the general fitness associated with good health.

Scholarship and Sport Culture

In the last 20 years there has been an explosion of scholarship associated with physical education and sport. One avenue of development has been the adoption of graduate status for schoolteachers, and another has been the application of science and technology in sport coaching.

As a result, there are academic qualifications available at many levels from examinations at 16+ through to doctorates. What differentiates the courses that lead to these qualifications from core curriculum physical education is an unashamed acceptance that a good part of the learning involved is concerned with scholarship. After a number of years of moderating and examining this work at 16+ to 19+, we see the essential difference between core curriculum and examination work as simply this. In the latter, in addition to their active participation in sport, students ask questions about activities and fitness and skill. They read books, invent games, do experiments, analyse videotapes, survey facilities, describe experiences and comment in essays upon issues of the day in sport and recreation. This surely is an important part of getting pupils inside the culture of sport.

Implications for Presenting Physical Education in the National Curriculum

Involvement with sport activity is our clear focus. However, we would make the plea that from the outset pupils are encouraged to categorize their activities into family groups in order to assist in making comparisons and reflecting upon experiences.

Such experiences are the foundation for later choices; hence, pupils should be building up resource bases to which they can later refer. Clearly, performance skills constitute an important part of this fund of information, but, as we have suggested, rules and the tactical aspects of performance are also important. As a pupil moves through the secondary years, we would suggest that the information relating necessary bodily conditions to activity demands is also relevant. Allied to this, each pupil should also understand the basis of the relevant anatomical and physiological principles. Senior pupils should surely be introduced to *concepts* of leisure and health-related fitness and, most important, should be taught about access to available resources.

Through the whole of the scheme, we would like to see pupils invited to explore alternative consumer roles and required to make judgements about them in the form of considered verbal or written answers.

Within all of this, there is considerably more demand for scholarship than within the average traditional programme, implying the need for pupils to have access to written material in books, handouts or worksheets.

Some of the work can and should be done in association with other departments. For example, there are obvious links with health education and biology. There are avenues of co-operation to be explored between physical education and dance and the other arts. Geographers and environmentalists have an important role to play in outdoor education. The English department can assist by using the experiences generated within our subject as a stimulus for creative writing, which can have a reciprocal purpose within physical education.

In all other subjects, pupils in school keep notebooks or work-files as resource bases for future work and reference. We see no reason why physical education should be any different. After all, teachers give out enormous quantities of information over the 5 or 6 years of compulsory secondary physical education, and it is clearly impossible for students to retain all of it in their heads. Critics of this idea say that it would detract from the time available for activity, that the children would therefore not like it, and that anyway they need a break from conventional teaching. We would reply by saying that we must differentiate between the educational business of the curriculum and the legitimate and necessary provision of recreation services to schoolchildren in extracurricular time. Having said that, we recognize that an effective yet workable balance between theory and practice must be achieved. This balance may vary both for children of differing abilities and at different stages of the physical education programme.

Conclusion for the Rationale for Physical Education

We conclude, therefore, that the essential focus for physical education in schools should be sport, defined in the widest possible terms. Our role should be to prepare children for sport culture within our society so that they may make best use of it in relation to their personal development, their effective use of leisure time and their physical and psychological well-being.

Aim and Long-Term Objectives of Physical Education

The rationale for physical education developed in this paper gives rise to a single overall aim and a series of related long-term objectives.

Aim: To transmit those aspects of our culture related to sport, broadly defined, and thus to develop within individuals a range of personal, social and scholastic qualities.

Objectives: To help young people

- become skilful, knowledgeable and discerning consumers of sport;
- acquire knowledge of health and exercise and adopt a healthy and active lifestyle through involvement in sport;
- acquire a positive body image and use their bodies skilfully and creatively in sport contexts;
- acquire a range of personal and social skills relevant to sport consumership; and
- gain qualifications and accreditation consonant with their intellectual and vocational aspirations.

The General Pattern of the Physical Education Curriculum 5 Through 16

The programme in schools must cater to children whose needs of it change as they grow older. We suggest that there should be four major stages in the National Curriculum for physical education.

Phase One (4 Through 7 Years): Mastery of Movement

This comprises the attainment of basic proficiency in a range of movement-skill categories that will provide the necessary foundation for later involvement in sport. In deciding what categories of movement to select, we should be aware of the scope of sport and of activities that young children are likely to wish to involve themselves in. We should also acknowledge that sometimes the resources required will lie outside the school, and sometimes in the home. These proficiencies are shown in Table 3.1.

The profession should develop expected progressions in these kinds of skills and publish relevant activity contexts that accentuate the essentially technical nature of learning for this age range.

Phase Two (7 Through 11 Years): Generic Sport Activity Experience

This is the development of technical skill and strategic awareness in the range of generic activities identified in the typology of sport on pages 45-48 (reproduced in Table 3.2). A generic activity is one that embodies the key characteristics within a category of the typology and that will provide a suitable context in which children can learn both the essential techniques of the activity type and how to apply them within the rules and strategic opportunities the activity offers.

In all these activity groups, teaching should seek a balance between the development of basic psychomotor proficiency and strategic awareness within the

Table 3.1   Proficiencies for Phase One of the Physical Education Curriculum

Proficiency category	Observable manifestation
Fundamental movement patterns	Running
	Skipping
	Stepping patterns
	Climbing
	Jumping for height and distance
	Jumping down
	Throwing for accuracy and distance
	Catching
Basic gymnastic skills	Balance
	Rotation
	Rolling
Basic dancing skills	Steps
	Body movement to music
Basic hitting skills	Striking and kicking stationary balls
	Striking and kicking moving balls
Swimming	Performing specified strokes
Roller-skating, ice skating, or skateboarding	Starting, stopping, maintaining
Bicycle riding	balance, negotiating turns

Table 3.2   Generic Areas of Experience for Phase Two of the Physical Education Curriculum

Sport category	Comment
Gymnastic activities	Include dancing.
Athletic activities	Include racing in a variety of contexts.
Conditioning activities	Emphasize experiencing the various effects of exercise.
New games	Emphasize the alternative features of these games.
Adventure activities	Introduce the challenge of this type of activity in rural and urban environments.
Field games	Emphasize skills involved rather than physical contact aspects.
Court games	
Net games	
Target games	
Innings games	
Fighting games	Exclude boxing for safety reasons.

operational context of generic rule structures. Children should be involved in the invention and modification of activities and in officiating. The mature sport forms as defined by the national governing bodies may frequently be unsuitable for core curriculum work. The 'teaching through understanding' method has demonstrated one approach to the development of a rounded appreciation of generic sport forms.

It is important that as the National Curriculum is developed for this phase, the profession takes note of two factors in deciding what the balance of the curriculum should be. First, the technical requirements of recognized gymnastic and (some) athletic activities are very sophisticated and beyond the capabilities of the majority of pupils. Second, there are many more activities in the games category than elsewhere. This is no doubt due to their essentially interactive nature and the fact that they can be enjoyably played at relatively low levels of skill. In selecting activities for inclusion in the programme, it would therefore seem that there is a need both to give pupils experience across the different categories of the typology and to weight that experience according to the attractiveness and relevance of particular groups.

Phase Three (11 Through 14 Years): Experience of a Representative Range of Sport Activities

This phase consists of a programme made up of activities selected from the various groupings of the previous phase (Table 3.3). The objective is to develop children's performance skills and awareness towards the level they will require for active involvement in community or representative sport.

Table 3.3 Examples of Phase Three Activities

Generic sport forms	Specific examples
Athletic activities	Track athletics
	Field athletics
	Cross-country
	Orienteering
	Swim racing
	Cyclo-cross
Gymnastic activities	Artistic gymnastics
	Rhythmic gymnastics
	Diving
	Trampoline
	Sport acrobatics
	Ice dancing
	Ballroom dancing
Conditioning activities	Aerobics
	Circuit training

(Cont.)

Table 3.3   (Continued)

Generic sport forms	Specific examples
Conditioning activities	Weight training
	Multi-gym
	Jogging
Adventure activities	Campcraft
	Mountaineering
	Canoeing
	Sailing
	Rock climbing
Field games	Hockey
	Soccer
	Rugby
	Water polo
Court games	Basketball
	Netball
Net games	Table tennis
	Badminton
	Squash
	Tennis
Target games	Archery
	Golf
	Darts
	Pool
	Bowls
Fighting games	Fencing
	Judo
	Wrestling
Field games	Rounders
	Cricket
	Baseball
	Softball
New games	Earthball
	Boffing Sticks
	Skinning the Snake

During this phase it is important that the selection of activities acknowledges national taste, local preferences and resource availability. Teaching methods should continue to ensure an integrated approach to tactical and technical skill development in relation to rule structures, along with modification of activities as appropriate for particular groups of pupils.

Phase Four (14 Through 19 Years): Physical Education for Life

We would suggest that during this phase there are three major themes appropriate to adolescents nearing the end of compulsory schooling and during the tertiary years. These are explained in Table 3.4.

Table 3.4 Appropriate Themes for Phase Four of the Physical Education Curriculum

Theme	Description
Leisure theme	Encourage pupils to develop existing skills and investigate new activities with a view to their adopting activities to continue outside and after school or college life. This would mean that pupils collect information about activity availability in the community and that professionals strengthen existing links between physical education departments and outside sports agencies.
Health theme	Give pupils an opportunity to engage in cross-curricular, health-related study and activity. Again, there are implications for links with agencies in the local community.
Vocational theme	Give pupils an opportunity to pursue examinable courses associated with sport as a logical extension of the programme in the preceding years. Such courses would include GCSE (General Certificate of Secondary Education) Physical Education at 16+ as well as the 'A' level PE/Sport Studies, City and Guilds 481 and BTEC (Business and Technician Education Council) Leisure courses available in the tertiary-age phase.

A characteristic of all three themes would be a greater emphasis on scholarship than in the earlier years of the programme. Courses should be designed to deliver the appropriate mix of hard knowledge, conceptual understanding and practical experience.

Should 4th/5th Year Physical Education Be Optional?

Two important and complex issues that the National Curriculum working party must address are whether the 4th/5th year physical education curriculum is compulsory or optional, and whether or not it should consist of a GCSE course. We would argue as follows. At the end of the third year of secondary schooling, and assuming the sort of programme 5 through 14 outlined here, pupils should know whether they have an interest in sport either as an examination subject or as recreative activity. Hence, the 4th/5th year curriculum programme should be optional.

The argument for educating pupils into the culture of sport underlines the relevance of physical education as a foundation subject in the National Curriculum.

The thematic approach outlined for Phase Four of the programme demonstrates that it is worth the 10% of curriculum time suggested for other foundation subjects. Pupils are expected to make a choice of seven or eight subjects from the foundation curriculum for GCSE examination. There is no earthly reason, in our view, why physical education should not be offered as one of those examinable subjects on a direct par with the others. We can see no justification for offering only a couple of periods of physical education a week to this age group. If it is really seen as foundation curriculum work, there is insufficient time (at only 5% of the timetable) to mount a course that will bear comparison with other foundation subjects, therefore conferring second-class status to physical education by default. If it is seen as recreation opportunity, then it does not deserve to be in the curriculum at all; schools should make appropriate provision for recreation of all kinds in extracurricular time.

We are forced to conclude, therefore, that physical education should seek full GCSE status for the 4th/5th year course, with a timetable allocation to match the other National Curriculum foundation subjects. This course would then be optional in the same way as the other foundation subjects. If the preceding programme and the design of the examination syllabus are appropriate, then GCSE should prove to be both educationally valid and extremely popular. This implies a thorough reappraisal of GCSE physical education since the existing courses have evolved piecemeal from experimental Mode 3 syllabi. The GCSE should be seen as the logical culmination of the staged progression in physical education we have identified.

The Extracurricular Programme in Physical Education

Much has been written about extracurricular physical education programmes. The most recent debate concerned the demise of competitive sport (though the issue was actually about representative sport) and the fact that fewer physical education teachers are now prepared to involve themselves outside normal school hours. Assuming that extracurricular programmes are set to continue, we should consider the basis on which they are to be organized.

Providing opportunities for children to engage in sport forms outside the curriculum ought to be part of a schoolwide policy for recreation. Local plans need to be developed to enable pupils to bridge the gap between school-based provision and the opportunities arising in the local community. A single school cannot hope to cater adequately for the range of sports pupils may elect to participate in. This implies a need for coordination between schools, sports clubs, local authority recreation departments and other sports bodies at local and regional levels. This liaison process needs to operate in two distinct modes: The talented pupil requires access to the best available training and coaching opportunities, while those whose aspirations in sport are more modest need to find an appropriate community setting in which to pursue their sports interests.

Conclusion

This paper constitutes an attempt at a rethink of the physical education programme in the context of the development and implementation of a National Curriculum. It is firmly based on the idea that education should be seen as preparation for life and that subjects within the curriculum should relate to identifiable cultural forms. Whilst we see sport, broadly defined, and its profitable use in leisure time as the cultural focus for our subject, we recognize its important contribution to the cross-curricular theme of health. We are concerned about the quality and commitment of physical education's recent involvement with dance as a part of the art culture, and we suggest that the performing arts are the proper context for this aspect of the child's education. Any teacher with a commitment to dance as art should find that setting the most effective in which to work, and training institutions should seek to provide that milieu for teacher education. We recognize that these views are at odds with many beliefs traditionally held dear by the physical education profession. However, the expansion of leisure time, the growth of sport as entertainment, its high profile in the media and the disappointing participation rates amongst school and college leavers all point to a need for a reassessment of our subject's aims and the strategies employed to realize them.

We have argued here for a progressive curriculum based on new thinking about the nature of sport activities and the range of consumer options open to young people. We see a need for the profession to identify its expectations of children in sport and to develop evaluation procedures that will enable teachers to assess the success of their teaching. We see a need for a greater degree of scholarship within the subject to enable pupils to understand the issues that impinge on their enjoyment of sport. Our thinking strongly supports the arguments for physical education specialists in the primary school.

We are committed to the notion of preparing young people to make the most of sport in their lives, and as such we would be happy to see the subject labelled 'Sport' or even 'Sport Studies' on the school timetable. There are those who would argue that this would devalue physical education because sport is perceived by many as something elitist and sensational. Perhaps that is precisely why we should *educate* our children about the *culture* of *sport*. The next generation of pupils might then leave school with a more enlightened and critical attitude towards sport and a greater enthusiasm to participate in it than is currently the case.

Appendix

Studies on the Value of Physical Education

HMI. (1979). *Curriculum 11-16 supplementary working papers: Physical education*. London: Her Majesty's Stationery Office.

Inner London Education Authority. (1988). *Our favourite subject. Report of a working party on physical education and school sport*. London: Author.

Murdoch, E. (1987). *Sport in schools*. Report of a desk study. London: Sports Council.

School Sport Forum. (1988). *Sport and young people: Partnership in action*. London: Sports Council.

Schools Council. (1974). *Physical education in secondary schools*. Report of a survey. London: Schools Council.

Schools Council. (1982). *Examinations in physical education*. Occasional bulletin. London: Schools Council.

References

Brackenridge, C.H., & Alderson, G.J.K. (1982). The implications of sport classification for sport science. In *Proceedings of the Sport & Science Conference* (pp. 2-14). London: British Society of Sports Psychology.

Bruner, J.S. (1972). *The relevance of education*. London: George, Allen & Unwin.

Cowie, E. (1983). Viewing patterns within the U.K. population. In *Annual Review of BBC Broadcasting Research Findings, 8*. London: British Broadcasting Corporation.

Hewlett, M. (1987). The explicit curriculum. *The Times* (Educational Suppl., January 2), p. 13.

Murdoch, E. (1986). Future trends in the physical education curriculum. *British Journal of Physical Education*, **17**, 83-86.

Parry, J. (1988). Physical education, justification and the National Curriculum. *Physical Education Review*, **11**, 106-118.

School Sport Forum. (1988). *Sport and young people: Partnership in action*. London: Sports Council.

Stenhouse, L. (1967). *Culture and education*. London: Nelson.

Wolfenden Committee on Sport. (1960). *Sport and the community*. London: Central Council for Physical Recreation.

Yates, A. (1984). *Final report of the Recreation Management Training Committee*. London: Her Majesty's Stationery Office.

Chapter 4

Physical Education and Sport: The Interface

Elizabeth B. Murdoch

During the last decade significant changes have taken place in the curriculum of physical education that have called into question yet again the relationship of physical education and sport. It is not proposed to rehearse the debate on sport in schools that has received such intense publicity in the last few years. What is important is to ask what, if anything, will emerge from that debate and what will be the nature and extent of the response to the pertinent reports that have been published (Department of Education and Science/Department of the Environment [DES/DoE], 1986; Greater London/South East Sports Council, 1986; Inner London Education Authority [ILEA], 1988; School Sport Forum, 1988; Southwest Council for Sport and Recreation, 1984; Sports Council for Wales/Welsh Council for School Sports, 1980).

The response to the debate within education has been temporarily overshadowed by the impact of the Education Reform Act of 1988 (DES, 1989) and the firm declaration in 1988 of physical education as a foundation subject within the National Curriculum. This must be welcomed by those in both physical education and sport because it secures for each child the entitlement of programmes of study and assessment schedules, at the same time confirming the importance of physical education in the eyes of educators, parents, governors, employers and the children themselves. It provides the basis for a new look at the interface of physical education and sport, a look that focuses on the needs of young people of today and the 1990s. There is opportunity now to put in place a statutorily required curriculum for physical education, and it is right that the interface between physical education and sport for children should exercise the minds of those preparing and approving the proposals.

There would appear to be a range of attitudes to the relationship between physical education and sport. These attitudes reflect the differing perceptions of the relationship between physical education and sport and give rise to questions that address this relationship as one that will offer mutual benefit and, more important, will ensure the best provision for each child.

Arising from these attitudes and perceptions, different models for this relationship will be proposed and discussed. Through this it will be seen that it is difficult to encapsulate the richness and complexity of the interaction between two such clearly established and distinct phenomena as physical education and sport. The issue will be addressed from the standpoint of physical education and 'new directions in the curriculum'. Each model will be examined in turn. They are not mutually exclusive in practice, but it is only by examining them discretely that the full relationship can be appreciated while preserving the distinctiveness of physical education and sport.

Can and should physical education serve the needs of sport as a cultural phenomenon? Should physical education educate for sport? Does sport provide a vehicle for physical education? These questions and others will be raised, and responses will emerge—if not explicitly, then implicitly—as the topic is explored.

The following models are proposed for examination:

- Substitution model
- Versus model
- Reinforcement model
- Sequence model

These arise from the ways in which the interface is perceived.

The first two models, *substitution* and *versus*, have negative connotations and do not hold potential for the development of working relationships. They are nevertheless significant in that they open up crucial and key issues that characterize many of the problems that the interface raises.

The *reinforcement* and *sequence* models, on the other hand, are positive attempts to capture the essence of somewhat uneasy but significant relationships that are seen to exist and considered worth developing. A further model, the *integration* model, will be proposed. It will address and attempt to provide for the many recommendations that are being made about sport in schools and its relationship to physical education within the National Curriculum, the full curriculum and the sporting community of which the school is a part.

The Substitution Model

'Sport and Physical Education are not the same' (School Sport Forum, 1988, p. C3.1). The need to state this firmly and often is felt by many in both physical education and sport. The refutation is made often in discussion with headteachers, teachers, governors, parents and children because many hold the view that physical education and sport are synonymous. When such a view is challenged, the holder is often willing to concede the error in principle but is neither able to analyse why this is possible or desirable nor to articulate the alternative. Much of the responsibility for the original misconception must lie with those who work in physical education and sport. The lack of clear statements of intent from either group gives rise to a real lack of understanding of what is the essence of each. This confusion is often reinforced by the interpretation of personal experience.

A recent broadcast was introduced by the presenter as 'School Sport, or to Give It Its Proper Title, Physical Education'. Such statements reinforce the urgent need for both physical education and sport to extricate themselves from the web of misunderstanding that reduces the influence of both on the lives of children.

The reasons for this 'substitution' can be understood in that traditionally the majority, if not all, of the physical education curriculum activities have been recognized sports; the child's initiation into these conventional sports has been seen by many as the raison d'être of physical education. What is overt and accessible to the observer looks very much like sport! The success of physical education programmes has been the success of the school teams. The strong historical tradition set in the public schools is replicated still in the minds of many and is hard to change.

The lack of written, easily available objectives related to curriculum planning, as well as the sports-oriented nature of the programme, has done little to contradict inaccurate assumptions of what physical education is about. The total ambience of physical education can be interpreted as sport, and physical education sessions carry many connotations of sport: The dress of participants, for example, is heavily reinforcing.

The confusion is understandable. Much is now happening that will call into question this substitution model, but the model is still significant in its impact on both physical education and sport. The fact of this confusion in the minds of many can be damaging: The claims that physical education would wish to be seen as an essential educative force in a child's development are often hard to substantiate when the curriculum and its delivery are seen to have many of the main characteristics of sport. The 'nonserious' nature of such an activity cannot be held up alongside the essential skills of numeracy, literacy and a knowledge of scientific concepts. This poses the teacher of physical education with a long, uphill run to reach the starting line—and how often do we use sporting analogies to make our points?

The implications of the substitution model are becoming more significant as the possible effects of the Reform Bill and other government legislation begin to become evident. The government has declared its intention to rationalize the forms of unusual entry to the teaching profession for mature students in the hope that for shortage subjects, at least, the numbers may be increased. The 'licensing' of teachers after a short period of training and experience in schools should give rise to some concern in the physical education profession because it will be possible, and not unlikely, that a mature entrant holding an impressive array of coaching awards may be seen by headteachers and governors as a highly suitable candidate for the teaching of 'sport'. After all, such people may have much higher sporting qualifications than a fully qualified teacher of physical education. The substitution model strongly reinforces this attitude. The possible effect of this on the profession and its supply of teachers is obvious and gives rise to some early concern.

It is necessary that, in their making provision for and in the resourcing of physical education, headteachers and governors are given clear mission statements from physical education and its relationship to sport so that simplistic interpretations of substitution are removed and that the differences between, and the real values of, both are understood. For the sporting bodies to reinforce the value they place on physical education for the child first and then for the sport would strengthen this understanding.

The Versus Model

There are differences between physical education and sport. The second model emphasizes what these differences are. There has always been a felt need to differentiate between physical education and sport, perhaps in reaction to the perceived substitution model in operation. In making distinctions the tendency is to state extreme, polar views. This strengthens the claims that physical education and sport are not one and the same and that sport cannot be a substitute for physical education.

There has been an uneasy relationship between physical education and sport in that sports clubs have been seen as a threat to physical education by putting pressure on young players to choose whom to represent, by setting what can be seen as dual standards, and by different patterns of behaviour. Sport has increasingly reported its unhappiness at the inadequacy of the physical education curriculum as a basis for sport at representative levels. Each has perceived the other as having different goals. This has reinforced the versus model (School Sport Forum, 1988, p. C3.2). Some of these polarities follow:

PHYSICAL EDUCATION	SPORT
Education	Recreation
Controlled by DES	Controlled by DoE
'New' physical education	Sporting competition
(led to media debate of 1986)	
Teachers	Coaches
Process	Product
LEARNING	PERFORMANCE
Child-centred development of the self	Sports-centred development of the sport
Participation and quality for all	Excellence for some
Compulsory	Voluntary
Ordinariness	Glamour

More pairs could be added! Reading down these descriptive columns does give 'definitions' of physical education and sport, but extreme interpretations are not helpful to future collaborative development. It is in the grey area between these poles that the real potential for co-operation lies.

The next three models address the collaboration and forms that it might take to ensure that the best of both is used for the benefit of the participants and performers. Talbot (1987) has reminded us that 'the game is not the thing, the child is'. The acceptance in both physical education and sport of such a spirit means there is a need to identify models of co-operation and collaboration based at best on common goals or at least on an acceptance of the merits of both sets of goals as a means to good provision for the children.

The Reinforcement Model

What is the place of sport in education? What is the role of education in sport? How do these coexist in the child's learning? The reciprocal nature of these questions gives rise to the proposal that physical education and sport can each reinforce the other's function.

> While training and coaching may be concerned with developing performance, education is concerned with developing people. However, there seems to be no reason why the two should be virtually exclusive; the training process can be educational if it is conducted in such a way that it contributes to the total development of the person. (Lee, 1986, p. 248)

Sport is used as one very suitable vehicle for physical education learning. The aims and objectives of physical education centre round the view that education must be about enhancing the individual in terms not only of knowledge and skill but especially of self-esteem and self-knowledge. Furthermore, each child is entitled to have a balanced range of experiences that ensure that he or she knows how to learn. These experiences are embedded in different contexts; one of these contexts is the area of sport through the involvement in specific sports.

Skilful teaching can ensure that, while the focus is on giving the child the appropriate learning experience, the integrity of the sport itself is not lost. The motivation to participate can be substantially increased by the sporting context. This demands that the teacher has a very clearly worked-out approach to the process of learning; the approach is of paramount importance and will be the basis of decisions. Appropriate selection of the sports will reflect the potential that each individual sport holds for the learning that has to take place.

Participation and performance in sports offers a number of valuable experiences that are central to a rounded education, including the following:

- The experience of competition and co-operation, and learning how to compete
- The concepts of winning and losing, and acceptance of both
- The concepts of failure and success, and acceptance of both
- The experience of preparation and training, and appreciation of their value
- The initiation into a cultural phenomenon, and its significance in our lives
- The preparation for spectatorship and sport analysis

So sport offers opportunity for essential and valuable educational experiences. These will not be revealed, however, to the participant without careful and systematic

tutoring from a teacher. These values have to be brought to the conscious awareness of the pupil before any claim for education in them or through them can
be made.

Sport holds potential for cross-curricular links. The expectation of the National
Curriculum is that a number of attainment targets should be linked with those
in other subject areas. For instance, there can be links with environmental studies
through the outdoor sports; links with sciences through nutrition, body and mental preparation and function; links with personal and social education through
the personal demands of sport and individual responses and resources. The approach of Technical and Vocational Educational Initiative (TVEI) to 'real-world
issues' in relation to sport as culture holds much potential.

There is no difficulty in making a case for sport to have a place in education.
As a vehicle for education, and particularly physical education, sport has a strong
claim.

Likewise, there is much that education can offer in the pursuit of sport by an
individual. Compiling a personal sporting profile can be of real value to a pupil
who is wishing to take part in sport. A study of body type and the relationship
of this to potential for success in specific sports can mean that many disappointments may be avoided by making correct initial choices. Ability profiles can help
the understanding of short- and long-term gains in performance levels. The notion
of plateaux of improvement and the changing profiles of abilities at different stages
of sport performance can become clearer. The study of diet and physical fitness
can enhance one's potential for success and significantly extend the satisfaction
gained from participation.

These and many other aspects of education have been well recognized by the
National Coaching Foundation in its Level 1, 2 and 3 courses for coaches. The
recognition of the need for education within coaching should result in more
thoughtful and appropriate coaching of the performer. The performer being able
to use this knowledge within his or her own context should increase the potential
for success.

More emphasis can be given to encouraging pupils to bring to the physical education context the needs of their personal participation in sport outside school
so that education and sport can exist alongside each other and be used to inform
each other. The coexistence of education and recreation carries great potential
for the furtherance of both by cross-reference, as exemplified by the following
quotation:

> There are examples of schools that have introduced the Community Sports
> Leaders Award Scheme (CSLA) into the school programme. This can involve
> collaboration with Colleges of FE [Further Education] and HE [Higher Edu-
> cation] and gives the pupil direct contact with the professional coach/teacher.
> (School Curriculum Development Committee [SCDC]/National Curriculum
> Council [NCC], 1989, Record 20)

The spotting of talented young performers within the education context should
be seen as a significant role for physical education. The potential for estimating

long-term possibilities for a pupil in a specific sport is great. Securing the appropriate outlet for such talent is also an important reinforcing role. Collaborative development between school and club in the interests of the pupil should be seen as very important and pursued where possible.

The small number of centres of excellence in Britain makes this task difficult. Because many local clubs do not have the resources to develop the talented young performers, the school is unable to relinquish direct responsibility. This creates a problem for the school—one that must be addressed if talented young people are not to be lost to the system:

Physical education looks after the child.
Sport looks after the game.
Together they look after the sporting future of children.

The reinforcement model raises many key aspects of the interface between physical education and sport. It consolidates a number of important actions that are being taken to make it possible for the benefits of physical education and sport to be mutually reinforcing.

The Sequence Model

'Physical Education should prepare young people for Sport.' The implication here is that physical education comes before sport in the sequence. It would be difficult to refute this in principle. What needs to be presented is a definite strategy for achieving this that is acceptable both to physical education and to sporting providers and consumers. This calls for a joint approach.

The sequence model focuses on the out-of- and postschool aspects of sporting involvement of young participants and performers. The target group for the Sports Council is ages 13 through 24, in the years of transition from school to the community outside school in the form of the other activity-providing agencies. It would be true to say that up until a few years ago, within physical education departments the approach to the problem of young people pursuing sport out-of- and postschool could be described as simplistic. The main way to implement the often occurring objective 'to prepare young people for participation in leisure' was to offer a range of experience of different activities in the hope that each young person would find something with which to identify.

It is safe to say that this was a false notion; many would now agree that it was. We know that participation by young people is closely related to success and satisfaction (White & Coakley, 1986; Williams, 1988). The following main reasons given by young people for feeling successful are related to motives and goals (Ewing, 1981; Whitehead, 1987):

- To show ability, often by being better than others
- To master an activity for its own sake
- To please others
- To feel a sense of adventure

- To do something not done before which one thought one couldn't do
- To achieve as a member of a team

Having fun is a constant must in teenagers' goals. Sadly the wide 'dip-and-taste' curriculum strategy that was adopted in many schools missed the mark in all these respects and could not hope to achieve its objectives of continuing participation.

There is a significant issue embedded in the first two of these listed reasons, seeking achievement and mastery. How can this be made available to young people—what does it mean—and are we anywhere near making it possible? These questions will be addressed in the section on the interaction model, but at this point it is important to stress that achievement and mastery do not appear after a short few weeks of exposure to a new activity. Too little is known about just how long it does take to reach a point of achievement in each sport and also how each sport will have a different time demand because of its intrinsic form and structure. There is much need for systematic research in this area.

We are beginning to address more fully the issue of preparing pupils for leisure and active lifestyles. It is assumed that participation and performance in sport is included in leisure and in fact plays a very large part in it.

A third dimension to participation and performance, which in Sports Council terms implies both activity and full involvement, is officiating in sport. This is an aspect that is underemphasized particularly in physical education, which understandably wishes to preserve its raison d'être, the *active* young person. Perhaps it is time to rethink the nature of the physical education programme for the later years in school and to consider the role of physical education in the preparation for an active lifestyle.

The Active Lifestyles project based in Coventry has developed in a very exciting way a new look at the preparation of young people for this active life. It has completely reset the programme for the upper years in school orientating it firmly to entry to the world of leisure and sport, addressing the skills and knowledge required not only to participate but, more important, how to gain entry to this world. The latter is seen as the greater stumbling block for many young people. It is encouraging that this project is continuing beyond its critical time scale and is giving us important information in terms of planning and feedback (Coventry Education Authority/Sports Council, 1985; Laventure, 1985).

A valuable Sportslink scheme has been set up, through Warren Wood Secondary School in Kent and involving the sports development officer, with a group of schools. Each school contracted into the scheme, which made available for each pupil the total experience of finding, setting up and taking part in the sporting provision of the local community (SCDC/NCC, 1989, Record 34).

Physical education as a profession has not yet universally taken on board the challenge of preparing its pupils for vocation within the areas of sport and leisure. Opportunities are available in the schools in the TVEI initiatives. Sport-related economic activity employs a significant proportion of our workforce in this country (almost 7%). The schools, and physical education departments in particular, have not yet fully investigated what this might mean in relation to preparation for employment. Much is to be learned from the further education sector in this regard. They focus on

- prevocational,
- vocational, and
- academic

as a basis for their courses having a specific focus. This structure offers a range of possibilities. The development of examinations in physical education, sports studies and dance is moving swiftly; these examinations will form a very firm base for young people to move into vocational outlets. The recognition of the examinations and their relevance both need to be constantly addressed by examination boards and the physical education profession so that they serve our young people as a basis for future academic and vocational progression.

Careers in sport are becoming available. Young people are interested. Schools must help, and new developments in the curriculum give a very good opportunity for this. The ILEA (1988) report *My Favourite Subject* has a specific recommendation calling for careers services to review the opportunities for employment in sport and leisure and provide advice for pupils.

An Integration Model

The four models thus far proposed and examined have reflected the existing varieties of approach and thinking about the interface between physical education and sport and have attempted to give some order to the complexity. None of these models individually, nor even an amalgamation of them, however, can provide the complete framework for the nature of relationship between physical education and sport for the 1990s. Some radical changes in practice in both physical education and sport are needed to meet the challenge of providing for the needs of each child. The integration model may be the mode in which those needs may be met.

There is enormous pressure on all providers of sport for young people to stand back and rethink their policies and practice. The main call is encapsulated in the title of the report from the School Sport Forum: *Sport and Young People: Partnership in Action*. The recommendations of this report address all who are involved in any way with sport for young people. The model that is implicit in these recommendations is an integration model. The main integrating force is the recognition that the child and the child's needs are the starting place. To implement this critically may require a change of attitude from all concerned.

The call is for coordination, co-operation and liaison, which inevitably will have a local and regional focus rather than a national one. It is only at the local level that the potential for a realistic and appropriate strategy can be found because no one pattern will be appropriate for all regions. It is acknowledged that because of the significance of school in the lives of children, what happens in schools is the key to the success of any integrated development. The integration model proposed will focus largely on the pattern of provision in schools and suggest how the relevant partnerships can be the basis of realistic objectives for the programme both in and out of school.

With the upheaval going on in the school curriculum as a result of 1988's Education Reform Act and National Curriculum changes there is great opportunity for changes in attitude and practice within physical education. This should make possible changes in attitudes and practice towards sport that will make partnership possible. If the opportunity is not fully taken now, a real chance for change and development will be lost.

The integration model is based on the following assumptions:

- We are addressing the age range of 'before 5 through 18 and after' *in continuity*.
- Young people are currently underachieving in both physical education and sport.
- No one agency can completely address the issues and offer independently any satisfactory solution.
- Physical education and sport should be integrated throughout the period of provision for the child from pre- to postschool and both in and out of school in the most appropriate way.
- The progress of a child through his or her education in the area of physical activity and sport must be developmentally smooth, and the responsibility for ensuring this should rest primarily with those in education. This does not mean, however, that only those in education can provide what the child needs.

Helping Primary Students Achieve in Sport

In the early pre-5 years, encompassing the transition into school, activity is high in a child's daily experience. This activity has a base in play and playfulness and will provide the child with satisfaction, a sense of achievement and fun. One has only to watch young children to acknowledge this. This must be preserved in the developing years, when the child becomes more and more competent and responds to increasingly difficult and sophisticated challenges both within and outside school.

The child will not develop from this early experience at an appropriate pace, however, if some structural support for learning is not available and sensitively used. Gradually each child is helped to master increasingly complex physical challenges in relation to his or her own level of competence. This requires very skilled observation and response by those working with him or her. It should be that by the middle years in the primary sector, each child is showing a sophisticated mastery of the fundamental patterns of movement and a sense of self-confidence born of that mastery. Both are essential as a basis for more specific learning and as an affirmation of each child's sense of worth. Each child by about 8 or 9 should be able to make consistently successful responses to novel tasks in unpredictable situations. The quality of these responses is also significant.

This may sound far removed from sporting achievement, and so it is in the formal sense. It is, however, the only foundation for sporting quality and excellence in later years. Without this base having been fully secured, the later developments are at risk. The child's sense of achievement is vital to future participation. Through this achievement comes satisfaction, which is the deep and lasting basis of enjoyment.

At present, this level of achievement is not realized in our primary schools. Appropriate experience is not being provided, and children are reaching later primary years sadly lacking in the mastery of their own bodies in movement that is their entitlement. We must acknowledge and accept this in education, and we must convince all those concerned that a real change must take place in this area. This has much wider implications than that of future sporting achievement because much is denied children through this inadequacy, and it is here that the seeds of both future participation and performance are sown. Equally, the attitudes that lead to dropping out are often set at this stage. Resources need to be made available in the shape of differently qualified teachers before this can improve.

If a strong foundation is secure, children in later primary and early secondary years can enter the more formal phases of participation in the activities of physical education and sport, moving from simple to complex versions. It is here that the integration of the work of the governing bodies of sport and of the National School Sports Association with education is essential. The development of mini sport forms is particularly significant and is proving very successful in making sport more accessible to children. Teachers and coaches can and should plan together to provide a rich and varied programme that addresses each child's needs in response to the challenge of a range of sports. Developing understanding of the complexities of competing and how to compete, and all the moral and ethical issues that this entails, would benefit from joint planning. It is important at this stage that common messages from sport and physical education are reaching the child through experts in both groups. While it is not possible and certainly inadvisable to attempt to place any age band on the development of a child's level of competence, there must be, for the sake of the administrative demands of schools, a series of points of change of emphasis that match as near as possible the developmental processes in children's learning. The advice of educators is paramount in this.

Continuing to Facilitate Achievement Through the Secondary Years

By the end of the first 2 years of secondary schooling, each child should be equipped to begin to select those sports that most suit personal needs and attributes and begin to take aboard the challenge of some in-depth experience in a few sports or even in only one. To effect this within a school timetable programme will pose problems, so the intention may not be fully achieved for all, yet the harnessing of as many resources as possible both inside and outside the school can go a long way to ensure that the programme for each child is as near the ideal as possible. A blend of school and club experiences that has a planned, combined focus—a programme negotiated by pupil, club and teacher—will avoid confusion and fragmentation of experience for the pupil. Each agency can take some responsibility for integrating the total experience for each pupil as far as possible. This describes an ideal situation—that is accepted, but it is the implication of following through an integrated model that focuses on the child and his needs. It is recognized that clubs do not at present have the resources or facilities to provide this support in full, but the raising of awareness may increase what is available.

If by the end of the 4th year of secondary schooling the pupil has had some in-depth experience of a few sports, then the nature and the level of the work done should be such that the pupil has a sense of self-satisfying achievement and has passed the early plateaux of lack of knowledge and skill that are the points at which many abandon the sport.

By this time early sporting talent should have been recognized, and those who have potential should have been integrated into a developed system appropriate to their potential. All pupils should have been able to extend their capacities as far as they wish and to recognize this. It is essential in the case of the gifted performer that the school makes an early recognition and has the contacts to promote this individual, supporting as and if necessary and being advised by the other agencies involved in a collaborative programme.

In the later years of secondary school, the pupils are in a position to consider courses that will offer them knowledge, understanding and experience that have both vocational and leisure orientations. For some this may mean examinations; for others it may mean the further developing of active lifestyles; for others it may mean in-depth development of known or new sports; and for others it may mean a focus on officiating. An imaginative programme is needed at this stage, where the school, the leisure and sporting industries, and the further and higher education institutions are collaborating to excite and encourage teachers and their pupils to prepare for leisure or vocation by considering the relevant issues. Such programmes can largely be designed by the pupils themselves, with teachers, coaches and others acting as consultants. The programmes thus negotiated may not focus on practical involvement for all pupils. If the 5 through 16 curriculum as outlined (Table 4.1) is in place, this should be a right and natural development for those whose talents will by now require specific outlets.

Making the Integration Model Work

The essence of this curriculum structure is its continuity. No one part of it can happen fully without all the others being in place. It all hinges on the early experience of children. If this is not right, the total programme is a catching-up exercise, and sometimes that is not ever achieved. The only guarantee for a young

Table 4.1   Model of the 5 Through 18 Curriculum in the Integration Model

Goal	Curricular provision	Age
Movement, play	Variety	Pre-5
Movement education	Width and variety of experience Deepening of skill	
Physical education	Conventional forms of activity Selection from range	
Education for leisure/vocation	Specialism	
Vocation/leisure		18 and beyond

Note. From School Curriculum Development Committee/National Curriculum Council (1988); School Sport Forum (1988)

person having a high achievement profile in secondary school is the early programme being in place. The reason for so many young people dropping out may be that they are delayed in their physical competence relative to their cognitive and emotional development, and this can cause tension and a sense of inadequacy not conducive to voluntary involvement. Any attempt to integrate physical education and sport must stem from a continuous process; anything less will mean that the focus will be on catching up, compensation and gross underachievement.

The following are the changes that need to take place to allow the integration model to work:

• *A new attitude within education accepts the input from the world of sport with a relinquishing of any feeling of threat*

• *A reappraisal of the content of physical education results in moving away from activity-based programmes of study to programmes that focus on different aspects of the child's learning process.*

This is under way in the National Curriculum. The potential of the National Curriculum programmes of study and attainment targets can open up possibilities for this integration model to be realized. All opportunities should be explored. Physical education and sport together can find within the personal and social education learning approaches an ideal base for many of the objectives each holds as important. The intentions and form of TVEI is highly compatible with the intentions of the integration model proposed. It is possible that in the future curriculum the time needed for physical education, so hotly debated, will not be found on all timetables as 'physical education' but may be there in a cross-curricular context. What must be preserved is the experience for each child.

• *The preparation of teachers both in primary and secondary sectors will need to develop and change.*

Those in the primary sector will require more and different experience. Those in the secondary sector ideally should have a range of skills, such as teacher/

primary consultant, teacher/coach, teacher/fitness consultant, or teacher/leisure adviser. This dual focus for teachers will make it possible for real integration to take place with the other agencies.

• *A joint in-service provision is called for so that teachers, coaches and leaders can work from a common base in relation to meeting children's needs.*

Teachers are calling for more governing body awards, while coaches are increasing, through the National Coaching Foundation (NCF), their awareness of the educational aspects of coaching.

• *A full understanding by parents, heads, governing bodies and children of the value of integrated planning is achieved, such that appropriate and sensitive support is forthcoming from all parties.*

If those in physical education and sport can make integration work, it may put pressure on those policy makers, administrators and providers to consider the resource problem as an integrated provision. Local authorities and even government departments should acknowledge that some cross-boundary discussion and action must happen between separate providing or managing groups, resources then being appropriately provided to support the developments.

There is only one way for the integration model to succeed, and that is for local and regional groups to meet and talk together. There is a significant role to be played here by the regional sports councils, who can stimulate 'Partnership in Action' through their membership. Greater liaison with education is needed, however, before this will have full impact.

The British Council of Physical Education and the Sports Council work closely through the Physical Education Advisory Group to come more closely together in terms of both policy and provision. As yet one of the major stumbling blocks to real integration is the fact of the separate departmental control of education (through DES) and sport (through DoE). At a local level this has real implications for the effecting of any joint policies and practices.

The most successful developments depend on and stem from small groups of committed innovators who can imaginatively overcome the apparent constraints that make integration look difficult. It is to these people, and there are many of them, that we owe acknowledgement for all the good practice that is in existence and through which we can be sure that many young people are having a satisfying experience within their sports both in and out of school.

References

Coventry Education Authority/Sports Council. (1985). *Education for an active life: Towards a relevant curriculum*. London: Sports Council.

Department of Education and Science. (1988). *Education Reform Act 1988 School Curriculum and Assessment. Circular 5/89*. London: Author.

Department of Education and Science. (1989). *From Policy to Practice—National Curriculum*. London: Author.

Department of Education and Science. (1989). *Personal and social education from 5-16* (Curriculum Matters 14). London: Her Majesty's Stationery Office.

Department of Education and Science/Department of the Environment. (1986). *Sport in schools seminar*. London: Department of the Environment.

Department of Education and Science/Welsh Office. (1987). *The National Curriculum 5-16: A consultation document*. London: Her Majesty's Stationery Office.

Ewing, M.E. (1981). *Achievment orientations and sport: Behaviour of males and females*. Unpublished doctoral dissertation, University of Illinois, Urbana-Champaign.

Greater London/South East Sports Council. (1986). *Physical education working party report*. London: Crystal Palace National Sports Centre.

Harrison, M. (1987). *The TVEI Curriculum 14-16: A summary*. Leeds: University of Leeds School of Education.

Inner London Education Authority. (1988). *'My Favourite Subject': A report of the working party on physical education and school sports*. London: Author.

Laventure, B. (1985). Linking school to the community—Setting the scene. *British Journal of Physical Education*, **18**, 60-62.

Lee, M. (1986). Moral and social growth through sport: The coach's role. In G. Gleeson (Ed.), *The growing child in competitive sport* (pp. 248-255). London: Hodder and Stoughton.

Murdoch, E.B. (1987). *Sport in schools: Desk study commissioned by D.E.S./D.o.E*. London: Sports Council.

National Council for School Sports. (1988). *Ideas on how to reverse the current decline in out of school activities*. Submission to the Ministers of Sport and Education. Unpublished.

School Curriculum Development Committee/National Curriculum Council. (1989). *Physical education: Recent curriculum developments*. London: School Curriculum Development Committee.

School Sport Forum. (1988). *Sport and young people: Partnership in action*. London: Sports Council.

South-west Council for Sport and Recreation. (1984). *From school to community: Report of a working party*. London: Sports Council.

Sports Council for Wales/Welsh Council for School Sports. (1980). *Working party on school sport*. Welsh Office.

Talbot, M. (1987). *Physical education and school sport into the 1990's*. Physical Education Association Fellows Lecture.

White, A., & Coakley, J. (1986). *Making decisions: A report*. London: Greater London/S.E. Region Sports Council, West Sussex Institute of Higher Education.

Whitehead, J. (1987). Why children take part. *Institute for the Study of Children in Sport Journal*, **1**(1), 23-33.

Williams, A. (1988). *Physical activity patterns among adolescents—Some curriculum implications* (Research Report). Birmingham: University of Birmingham.

Chapter 5

New Directions in Games Teaching

Rod Thorpe

Sport is a significant part of our culture, and 'games' are a major part of the sport that people play and see in all forms of the media. It is not the intention of this article to debate the wisdom of this but rather to start with the assumption, naive and biased perhaps, that a games experience presented well can be enriching for anyone and should be included in the curriculum. It is the opinion of the author that a meaningful games experience will be achieved only if it is progressive (preferably from ages 5 through 16) and planned with opportunities to learn and play in the wider community considered; inevitably, many of the games experiences will occur outside the curriculum.

Almost by definition the physical education specialist should be trained to recognize the relationships between different games and between the games and other activities of the curriculum. The physical education teacher should be able to justify games as a medium in which to give responsibility, to investigate working with others, to allow problem solving and to encourage communication skills, trust, co-operation, coping with disappointments and so on. Many teachers of personal and social development search for games (in the wider sense) that allow them to investigate these issues; the physical education teacher has them ready to hand. The physical education profession must not consider itself to have a monopoly on caring about and the development of these wider aims, either in the school or in sport, but it is shortsighted to prepare games programmes that do not have these issues as central considerations. Finally, it would seem that physical education specialists should recognize, and not merely pay lip service to, their wider role as managers of games experiences for young people. The argument is made that the political climate is right for a review of both the games curriculum and the interaction between school and the wider community.

The intention of this chapter is to look at recent debate about games in the physical education programme, to focus on the quite different problems to be found in presenting a games programme in the primary and secondary sectors and to consider the relationship of the physical education games programme as central to a wider but more coordinated games experience. The chapter will then go on to look at the sort of games education that might be offered within the physical education curriculum to provide both a sound educational experience in its own right and a base from which to move into sport at any level. Throughout is sounded a plea to recognize that the physical education teacher is only one of a number of individuals who provide the games experience for children and should, rather than see 'others' (e.g. leaders and coaches) as threats, play a central part in defining roles the others might play. If the games programme is merely a series of separate games taught with the intention of producing good performers, then coaches may be better able to meet this need, and physical education teachers should accept this. But this author and many others have for a number of years been suggesting that a games education should be so much more and that physical education teachers have a unique role to play in it. It is as important that physical education teachers can explain their own unique role in a games education as it is that they define the role of others.

Games in the Physical Education Programme

Whilst suggesting that a games experience presented well can be enriching, it is not intended to be implied that games, particularly certain types, should take a disproportionate amount of time in the physical education programme. According to Williams and Jenkins (1988), 'Unfortunately most of the available evidence suggests that while the curriculum offered is frequently broad, it is rarely balanced, with team games continuing to dominate' (p. 112).

Murdoch (1987), in her review of literature concerning the attitudes of young people to participation and sport, points out that there are 'tensions between [young people] and the providing agencies especially in traditional expectations about competitive team sports. . . . There is a growing tendency in young people to be going for more individual sports or those for small groups' (p. 13).

There are also considerable concerns about the way in which the games programme is presented. The Physical Education Association (PEA) (1987) points out that there is evidence of games teaching where supervision rather than dynamic teaching occurs. One has to question the need for a physical education teacher in such circumstances.

Games lessons can appear to progress fairly well with only a modicum of input from the teacher (hence the greater traditional acceptance of untrained teachers into this area of the physical education programme than into any other). There may well be a tendency to include a disproportionate amount of games simply because it works with little effort from the teacher. It might be that teachers feel that some learning and valuable activity occurs within this structured play environment.

These statements might lead to certain questions:

• Do teachers offer a disproportionate amount of time to certain types of games because they are easy to 'teach'? If these games are offered as separate entities,

could the children gain valuable experiences from a combination of coach
and leader, the former to provide progressive learning experience and the
latter to provide the structured play?

- Assuming that most physical education teachers offer games for other reasons
  than ease of teaching, what is the games experience that the child should
  receive in the physical education lesson, and why is the physical education
  teacher uniquely qualified to deliver it?

- Recognizing that the physical education staff cannot provide the total games
  experience, how might the physical education teacher manage the resources
  (people as well as facilities) available in the community (including the school)
  to provide this wider experience?

Such questions cannot be resolved without entry into the far larger debate of
the future roles to be played in a child's games experience by the physical education
teacher, the sports coach, the sports leader and so on. In attempts to clarify these
roles, the profession has encountered some difficulty because often the physical
education teacher is a coach and takes on a coaching role in which improvement
of performance is the central aim. This possibly happens more in games than
in any other area of physical education. Murdoch (1987) highlighted 'the need
to clarify the role of the teacher of physical education and that of the coach attached
to a local club' (p. 15).

This may appear to be irrelevant to discussions about games in the physical
education curriculum, but it is the author's belief that by identifying more clearly
the different roles these individuals can play in the total games experience, it is
possible to identify the unique role the physical education teacher can and perhaps
should play. In an attempt to clarify the roles when discussing leadership, the
author used the example of tennis (Thorpe, 1988). A similar approach might help
here.

As a parent, if I send my children to a tennis session run by a leader, I would
hope that they would play appropriate games and perhaps do fun practices.
I expect my children to be safe, to have a fair number of 'gos' and so on.
The main skills the leader might exhibit are good organization and clear
communication, coupled with a pleasant, enthusiastic manner. I would not
expect progressive teaching.

Should I send my children to a coach, I would expect the coach to improve
their performance. Clearly, the coach must have the particular and specialist
knowledge of tennis and a basic knowledge of child development. I would
expect to see long-term training programmes that consider technical, tactical,
physiological and psychological aspects, good analytical skills and so on.

Should the physical education teacher present tennis (I realize this may not
be possible in some circumstances, but I would expect to see a divided court
game of some sort), then I hope it is offered in a way that helps my children
to understand the tactics, to recognize why certain rules are necessary and

to work with other children to solve the problems posed by the game. I hope there will be options of equipment so that if they are somewhat inept, they do not feel incompetent (a sponge ball might help); but if they are good, they can test themselves. I do not expect the physical education teacher to improve my children's backhand significantly, but I will object if they waste time relearning a skill mastered several years earlier. I expect the teacher to justify why they are doing tennis at this time in the physical education programme, how this game might help my children understand volleyball and what exercise effect the game might have. Finally, I expect the physical education teacher to tell my children where they can go to play tennis and similar games (particularly if they have not been taught in the physical education lessons) and where they can gain specialist tuition.

The Primary Sector

The use of the term *physical education teacher* tends to focus the debate on the secondary school, but what of the primary sector? Despite the general belief that the years up to 11 are vital to the development of basic movement patterns and, perhaps more important, to the development of attitudes toward physical activity, there is little specialist knowledge available to the primary school. Reviewing the work of Cadman (1980), Campbell (1986) and the PEA (1987), Murdoch (1987) was led to report,

> It is acknowledged by all parties both in education and in the sporting world that the training of the teacher in Primary School is not adequate in most instances for the complex task of giving children a sound movement/physical education. (p. 21)

Getting Help

The physical education fraternity should not be surprised if the managers of primary schools look for help outside the teaching profession. Just as primary school headteachers invite adults into school to listen to children read, so it seems logical to extend this invitation to knowledgeable adults and/or sports leaders to *assist* the classroom teachers in the games lessons. Of course, the physical education teacher who hears of a sports leader (with approximately 20 hours training) *taking responsibility* for a primary class physical education lesson has every right to be concerned, but this should not blind the profession to these facts:

- Having an enthusiastic, *appropriately trained assistant* would be a great benefit to many teachers in the primary sector.
- These individuals bring to the lesson more enthusiasm and often more knowledge of the activity being taught than the class teacher.

Few would dispute the fact that having an enthusiastic model is a major factor, particularly at the age when imitation plays such a major role in learning. Indeed, the first 'general recommendation' of the Inner London Education Authority

(ILEA) Schools Working Party (1988) is for 'enthusing and informing the young about physical activity to be the top priority for teachers of Physical Education' (p. 84).

Before criticizing the headteacher who allows a sports leader to take responsibility for a games lesson, it is important that the physical education profession identify what it is in this situation that we object to. It is insufficient to say that the person is undertrained, having accepted for years that most primary teachers have less than 60 hours in their initial training allocated to the *whole* of physical education (Williams, 1989). Whilst accepting that the primary teacher has a knowledge of child development that the leader may not, few would deny that the games experience offered to many primary children is inadequate and often inappropriate. Of more concern is that primary school teachers report having insufficient knowledge, confidence or experience to present games in a way that allows them to meet the developmental needs of the child. Knowledge of child development does not necessarily transfer to the practical lesson.

No criticism of the teachers is intended. Mrs Peggy Thomas (1988), a Leicestershire primary school headteacher, reflecting on her observations of primary physical education, alerts us to the problems. She said, 'Many students and teachers *lack confidence* in their ability to teach P.E. properly. They often express feelings of inadequacy in this area of the curriculum, they may be excellent teachers in other respects' (p. 7). And this lack of confidence, once rooted in the school, perpetuates the problem.

A student/probationer learns a great deal from experienced teachers when in school. However, because of lack of real expertise and understanding of the subject in many primary schools, many teachers have evolved their own survival technique and P.E. lessons can lack the element of challenge, stimulation and enthusiasm necessary to promote sound development of skills and abilities. (p. 7)

Recognizing Problems

Any development of a games education for ages 5 through 16 must recognize the problems faced by those presenting the programme. It is the author's experience that primary teachers can see the educative possibilities in the games experience with a relatively short course directing attention to the issues. However, they need considerably more help in identifying the learning objective, the appropriate game form* and, more particularly, the basic organizational skills to run the lesson.

---

*In a games programme a variety of forms of game must be used if the learning outcomes are to be achieved. If the intention is to present a game to primary children that looks like the adult game, a 'mini game', e.g. kwik cricket or short tennis, might be used; but adult game patterns are often inappropriate. Some forms of game stress a physical movement pattern, others help the understanding of a tactic and yet others present vehicles for co-operation or competition. Primary teachers use adult games perhaps because they have not been introduced to the different forms of game available or do not understand how to modify and develop games.

Most people who have wrestled with the problem of games in the primary sector will have met a comment similar to this:

> I can see the logic in small sided games but how do you get them started and how do you cope when there is a disagreement? It's so much easier to have one big game—the children are not rushing about. (Current Post Graduate Certificate of Education [PGCE] primary student, personal communication)

Possible Solutions to the Need for Better Games Programmes

If this is such a vital stage of children's development, it would seem essential to provide possible answers to these problems. The National Curriculum will give impetus, but the answers must recognize the realities. Several things can be done to improve games programmes in the primary school. The following list summarizes a few possible solutions.

• *Priority of in-service training.* The ILEA report 'My Favourite Subject' (1988) clearly identified that priority of in-service training (INSET) should be given to primary teachers. Until there are confident teachers of physical education in the schools, the probationary teacher will find it difficult to find help.

• *Realistic training.* Clearly, the physical education profession should argue strongly for more initial teacher training time to be allocated to physical education. In the meantime, though, it may be that a little less time has to be given to the educational 'niceties' and more given to (a) the organizational 'tricks of the trade,' e.g. showing teachers how to introduce small-side games to small groups within large lessons, and (b) designing a games programme based on tried and tested games (appropriate to the age and development of the children in the class) that in themselves present a series of progressive problems for the children to solve through assisted play. The in-service games days offered to Leicestershire teachers have in recent years taken this realistic approach. Teachers have been shown and have shared games that work. If the children are involved in the games and the organizational problems are met, the teachers have time to consider the educational themes they wish to develop. More time should also be spent presenting games that do not need high levels of co-operation to children who have not yet learned how to work together.

• *Welcoming help from appropriately qualified others.* Whilst acknowledging the problems, this author is excited by the fact that a few selected sports leaders might spend some time helping in a primary school. I can see no reason why the trend to invite parents in to help with the children's education should not be extended to physical education (safety not withstanding). What a difference it would make if parents went home to play and exercise with their children as well as to read with them. Would it be difficult to run sports leaders courses for parents?

• *Partnerships between secondary and 'feeder' primary schools.* This is not always easy organizationally or at the personal level, but it is essential if a 5 through 16 programme is developed.

- *Curriculum leaders*. This is a major issue beyond the scope of this chapter, but it is difficult to see how a school can provide a physical education programme without some specialist input.

It would appear that the primary child's games education is less than ideal. It may be that the National Curriculum will provide the impetus to clarify both the desirable outcomes of the physical education programme and the means to achieve them.

The Secondary Sector Physical Education Teacher, One of a Team

The term *games experience* has been used intentionally to reflect the author's personal belief that the teacher of games should not be narrow when planning the games programme for his or her children but should consider the whole social environment in which the child develops. This is as important in the secondary school as in the primary school. It would appear that the days are gone, in most schools, when the physical education teacher could expect several staff members to help with school teams. Whilst debate has often concentrated on the willingness of teachers to give of their time, it is worth seriously considering whether the classroom teacher is now qualified to take activities in which inappropriate methods could lead to injury. The physical education teacher, as guardian of the games programme, might reasonably question the hitherto common practice of leaving children with the knowledgeable but untrained helper, which might include the willing schoolteacher as well as the sports leader.

Partnership in Games Teaching

It follows, therefore, that a full range of games experiences will not be possible if the opportunities are restricted to the school environs or to activities offered only by 'qualified' schoolteachers. Whilst it could be argued that the family and the peer group have always been important in providing the games experience, in the past the schoolteacher has been seen as the main, if not the only, trained provider of structured games experiences for most children.

It is important to recognize that this may not be the case in the future. The report from the School Sport Forum (1988) draws attention to the advantages to be gained from recognizing the partnerships that can contribute to the sport experience of children. Games are certainly an element of the physical education programme that can make full use of such initiatives. The ILEA report (1988) presents quite specific recommendations about these links in the sections 'School Sports Associations' (Rec. 50-56) and 'Co-operation between School and Community' (Rec. 57-61).

Campbell (1988), in outlining what the 'sport lobby' demands of initial teacher training, made the following observations:

I believe that the physical education teacher should be the custodian of the curriculum programme but I do believe that there is a place for *appropriately* qualified assistance to be used. . . . It is vital that physical education takes a more proactive role in sport and becomes politically more aware. (p. 22)

Games is an obvious area in which the partnerships identified can operate, but to control this partnership and make best use of the contributors, the individual physical education teacher must look outside the school. In the future the head-teacher with control over finance may well ask some searching questions about who supplies the games experience; buying in a coach will be cheaper than employing another physical education teacher. The physical education profession should not wait for things to happen but should decide what should happen and present the case. The ILEA report and the School Sport Forum are excellent starting points.

Responsibility for Extracurricular Activity

If the curriculum is still seen as the domain of the physical education teacher, then responsibility for extracurricular activity is not. 'Extracurricular' here means all activities outside the curriculum, including out-of-school activities, because it is the author's belief that this distinction will rapidly disappear. Games will be offered on school grounds by people other than teachers; teachers will continue to coach their pupils with others in clubs out of school.

Irrespective of the accuracy of the many arguments about the degree of extra-curricular involvement of teachers and children in games, there is evidence that bodies traditionally seen as peripheral to the educative side of children's sport, e.g. the sport governing bodies, leisure services, local sports clubs, Sports Council, and Youth Service, have come to realize that it is important to look to the school-aged youngster. Many local education authorities employ dual-use advisers; some are refocusing attention from mere facility sharing to look at realistic ways of using teachers and coaches in more efficient ways (Dickenson, personal communication, 1989). School governing bodies, with their increased managerial powers, must look at facility use and may turn first to the head of physical education. Are physical education teachers ready to propose the sort of use of the facilities that will ensure the children a fuller games experience?

Some in physical education see these developments as a real danger, recognizing that the sort of ethos set in some sports clubs and the values held by some sports coaches are incompatible with those presented by the school. These teachers may be unaware of the efforts being made by the National Coaching Foundation (NCF) and governing bodies to ensure that coaches have a real understanding of the needs of children. There is still evidence, however, that the answers proposed by the governing bodies do not always meet the needs of the teacher and pupil in schools. The movement toward skill-based award schemes for games like association football and tennis are, in the opinion of this author, quite inappropriate for the games curriculum. Others have discussed the dangers inherent in offering extrinsic rewards to activities that are in themselves intrinsically motivating (Biddle, 1986; Weinberg, 1984).

Yet, these same governing bodies have done much to aid development of games for children. It was in soccer that were first articulated the principles of play that many of us now use to provide a framework for the development of an understanding of games (Wade, 1967). The Lawn Tennis Association (LTA), by the development of a Short Tennis Leaders Award, has recognized the need to provide a game that children 'can' play and helpers to provide the opportunity 'for' play. Whilst these developments and many like them in other games move sport nearer to children, they do not provide the answer to the games curriculum.

The Need for a Coherent Approach

I firmly believe that there should be a coherent games education, offered in the school physical education programme, that takes children from 5 to 16 years of age, recognizing their mental, social and physical development. This coherent approach, which requires the teacher to move more logically from one game to another than hitherto and is far more than a series of separate games experiences, has been described elsewhere (Thorpe & Bunker, 1989). The implication of such an integrated games programme, which meets the wider aims of education and draws on related work from other areas of physical education, is that it must be taught by the fully trained physical education teacher. It is important to state at this time, because misunderstandings easily arise, that this does not mean flitting from one game to another. It may mean that a valuable games foundation would have young children play games that as yet only vaguely resemble any adult form, but this is followed by a movement toward a sampling of games that are studied for some time. There is some evidence that it is unnecessary, and perhaps undesirable, to try and teach everything.

The width and depth argument has been discussed elsewhere concerning other areas (Murdoch, 1987), but there is a major difference in the area of games. There are considerable commonalities between games, and a games programme can be taught in a way that allows children to understand a range of games at least at a basic level. If these same young people are confident of their own ability to participate in these games, they may need only the opportunity to move into other activities. That this could happen against a background of co-operation with trained coaches and leaders seems exciting. It will not be easy to develop a complete network of extracurricular sport opportunities, and each area will differ dramatically. The problem is that 'the sports system consists of hundreds of public and tens of thousands of voluntary and commercial operations, most fairly small' (Smith, 1980, p. 7).

This situation may not remain; responses to a consultation paper on sports leadership (Thorpe, 1988) indicate that local authorities would welcome a more coordinated approach to sport provision.

There is a belief that the Association should support the desire for Community Sports Officers to make links between school and community programmes. (Association of County Councils, 1988, p. 67)

We need to begin by identifying the needs of people of all ages and abilities, both in the school and in the community. School-based physical education programmes have played, and must continue to play, a central role in every child's education. However we should also recognise the growing requirement to provide a more systematic, well-structured and competently staffed community-based programme of sport and recreation. The training of leaders, coaches and teachers has to be considered in the context of a common, corporate framework, so that both human and physical resources can be effectively utilised. The employment and deployment of leaders, coaches and teachers will vary locally but should operate under an agreed set of principles. (Association of Metropolitan Authorities, 1988, p. 62)

Once again the ILEA report (1988) indicates possible ways forward by concluding that 'every Secondary School [is] to designate one teacher with responsibility for leisure liaison with outside bodies' (p. 85) and 'School Sports Associations [are] to seek liaison with Borough Sports Development Officers' (p. 86).

It may be that employers (local authorities, holiday firms, sports clubs, youth clubs) employing coaches to work with children should demand evidence that the coach has at the very least been alerted to the dangers of inappropriate coaching of youngsters. An NCF Level 2 course might be a minimum requirement. The programmes are now available and offered throughout the country.

If those in the physical education profession see themselves as guardians of the child's games experience, it might be that they accept the advice to be more proactive and help formulate the recommendations to guide the training and coordination of leaders and coaches working with young children. This would seem to imply that the physical education teacher must look carefully at two quite different roles as provider of the total games experience: first, the role as a coordinator, manager, and facilitator of appropriate games experiences and, second, as the designer and provider of the games education that all children receive in the physical education curriculum.

Extracurricular Games

I do not feel the physical education profession should now abdicate responsibility for the wider games experience, for a number of reasons, including the following:

- The school is a relatively safe environment.
- Staying on after school or playing at lunch time is far more convenient than having to make another journey to a sports club. Certain children may be unable to make the additional journey. (The ILEA [1988] recommends the development of school sports centers open at weekends and during the holidays as well as after school.)
- Some element of control can be maintained if the games experience is offered within the school or local authority system.
- The sports club network (as on the continent) is not yet in place, and the external sports club might demand a financial commitment that cannot be met.
- The physical education teacher has been trained to offer a games experience to this age of pupil.

- The physical education teacher has experience of designing material for different abilities and needs.
- The physical education teacher should be sensitive to the overall balance of the child's games experience and so on.
- The physical education teacher can use this extracurricular experience educationally.

Teachers' Roles in Extracurricular Games

Of course the teachers' action and the subsequent teachers' contract have caused a number of physical education teachers to consider their personal roles in extracurricular games provision. The subsequent return to 'normal' practice has been quite varied: Some teachers immediately restarted their extracurricular programmes unchanged, others took the chance to try different approaches to extracurricular experiences, and yet others took the point of view that offering this form of experience was not in their contract. Games is a major area of physical education affected by these changes. The English Schools Football Association (1988) reported that over half their members felt the teacher's contract had affected school football, and a quarter felt that this had affected school representative football.

The production of excellence, the concern expressed by the representatives of traditional team games that the schools are failing to nurture the next generation of players in these games, the value of competition and so on enter the debate at this point, but these arguments have been rehearsed elsewhere (Murdoch, 1987). It seems to this author futile to make comparisons with the past, when young people had less conflicting leisure activities, fewer sports competed for time, and it was possible to play to a reasonable standard in many sports with a minimum of structured training. We can learn much from the past, but we must develop a structure for the future.

The Nature of the Extracurricular Activity

Before moving to the curriculum programme, it is necessary to question a few assumptions. Cockerill and Hardy (1989) cast doubt on the simple assumption that extracurricular activities in a school increase participation levels.

Some teachers offer a games programme designed to meet the needs of all abilities but then offer an extracurricular games club to which only the team members are invited and in which the teaching is presented with far more enthusiasm. Such a teacher cannot realistically expect the children to perceive him or her as centrally interested in improvement, commitment and knowledge rather than absolute performance. It may be that what some have called the extended curriculum, i.e. those experiences offered and promoted by the physical education department as an extension of the children's education, should be available to all. These extended curricular activities may or may not be competitive, dependent not on the physical education department's philosophy but on the needs of the children. The fact that the games for the selected few are thus distanced a little from the curriculum and are not seen as the central role of the physical education teacher might help overcome some of the negative affects identified earlier. The wider issues of extracurricular provision have been discussed in *My Favourite Subject* (ILEA, 1988), *Sport in Schools* (Murdoch, 1987), *Sport and Young People* (School Sport Forum, 1988) and 'School Sport in Great Britain' (Chappel, 1989).

The physical education teacher as provider of this wider games experience might consider running sport leadership courses for parents and older pupils; many governing bodies now offer short courses designed to be completed in one day*. A few candidates may then wish to move on to coaching awards, but many could be quite happy working within the extended curricular or extracurricular programme.

How often do teachers consider what is available in the community and how they might support it? In games, there is certainly the problem that ease of access to competitive play lies with the talented. The basic philosophy of 'teaching for understanding' (discussed in detail later) is that a person can play games with limited techniques and, even with limited techniques, can be very competitive. A danger in a more balanced games programme, designed to alert a wider range of children to different forms of games, is that there may be few opportunities for them to play. The physical education staff may have to weigh up a number of issues; a conversation might run as follows:

'We know there is an excellent club junior soccer league in our area, run by people well aware of the needs of young children. We could support this and encourage our competitive, talented youngsters to join (we must remember to submit the best youngsters for the school's county trials). This gives us time to run an all-welcome soccer session on two evenings in which there will be the chance for competition. . . . There are no basketball clubs in the area, and I know a number of schools use basketball in the curriculum. Shall we run an interschools tournament on one Saturday morning and assess the interest?'

Offering basketball instead of soccer would be a hard decision to make if the school had a strong reputation for soccer, even when that strength came from the community soccer programmes. Does pride lie in the school team or in the achievements of the youngsters? It may be that—like the Active Lifestyles Project in Coventry, which has the support of local education authorities, other local authorities and the Sports Council and brings many of the agencies for sport together—certain initiatives may enable the school to take pride in community sport.

Interschool sport has provided the nursery for many talented games players; it is quite inappropriate to disband it until there is an acceptable alternative. It may be, however, that in many games it is too restrictive for the development of the talented. It is equally unrealistic to expect the physical education staff to offer the width that might be demanded. The situation is complex, but the new direction in extracurricular games opportunities appears to lie with a better coordinated

---

*Information about such courses in England (and, in some cases, the UK) are available from the Central Council for Physical Recreation (CCPR) in London.

use of various agencies, and the physical education teacher could well be the manager of that network.

The Games Experience in the Curriculum

Physical education professionals have to decide what games experience they feel should be offered to all children in the curriculum. The debate about the National Curriculum should speed this process.

Many of us are confident that it is possible to teach games in a way that can give children of *all abilities* success, knowledge and interest. However, it is important to recognize that games lessons can also be places of embarrassment and physical discomfort and can serve to convince the participant of his or her incompetence. This concern should not be overstated, however, in that the general impression gained from recent reports is that the vast majority of children enjoy the physical education lesson—which is not quite the same as enjoying the subject (Dickenson & Sparkes, 1988; ILEA, 1988)—and that 49% of boys and 35% of girls preferred games to alternatives classified as individual activities, fitness activities and water activities (Dickenson & Sparkes, 1988*). The gender differences would seem to support an impression gained by the author, when taking in-service courses, that teachers see a greater need to review the games experience offered to girls than that offered to boys. It is worth remembering that games might be successful, particularly with boys, despite rather than because of the teacher or the approach. Children, particularly boys, play games in the absence of both guidance and extrinsic motivators.

Taught well, the area of games presents an excellent medium in which to use different teaching styles and approaches, which ensures that the many more general aims of education, often embraced by terms like 'personal and social development,' can be met. It is important that we present games in a way that meets the needs of the young player. Incentives frameworks provided by sports psychologists, such as self-direction (Csikzentmihalyi, 1975), affiliation, excellence, stress, and success (Alderman & Wood, 1976)—expressed slightly differently by the coaching world as affiliation, achievement, sensation and self-direction (Coaching Association of Canada, 1972)—can provide a start. It may be necessary to modify these to meet the needs of the very young (Whitehead, 1988).

It may be that there are some principles that can guide an essentially child-centred presentation of a games programme. Almond (1989) proposes that the following key components are necessary:

- Learning from doing
- Sharing in learning
- Ownership of learning
- Independence

---

*It should be noted that this study did not restrict games to 'major invasion games' and is thus not at conflict with earlier observations about attitude to traditional games.

It is important, therefore, that any content selected must be presented in a way that facilitates these outcomes. Thus, if a child is to feel 'ownership of learning', the teaching style adopted will be quite critical.

Those of us who have been central to the 'teaching for understanding' approach to games believe that it can provide both a philosophy for, and a working model to meet, the requirements of a games education. It has been designed against a background of the issues already presented above, e.g., (a) it capitalizes on the intrinsic motivation inherent in games and proposes the inclusion of skill work only when the need is recognized by the child; (b) it leans heavily on guided discovery and problem solving, so the ownership of the answer to the problems posed by a game lies with the players (it is the opinion of the author and co-workers that because games present a series of problems, these styles of teaching are far easier investigated in games than in 'educational gymnastics'); (c) whilst it focuses on knowledge and understanding, these are gained through practical experience; and so on.

Furthermore, this education prepares the young person to appreciate and participate as player, spectator or administrator in games outside the physical education lesson.

Teaching for Understanding

The development of this approach has taken many years (Thorpe, Bunker, & Almond, 1986). Its validity has been tested in the following ways:

- In direct comparison with more traditional methods by students (from Graham, 1971, at the exploratory stage to Lawton, 1987, more recently)
- In direct comparison with more traditional methods by practising teachers (Almond & Thorpe, 1988; Coventry teachers, 1986)
- By examining the procedure against current theory in the areas of skill acquisition, sports psychology and sports pedagogy; some of these links have been outlined elsewhere (Pigott, 1982; Thorpe, 1989)

Even so, by far the greatest insights and modifications have resulted from discussions and ideas presented by colleagues, teachers, students and so forth.

Introduction to the Teaching for Understanding Approach

It is not the intention in this chapter to reiterate work presented elsewhere but merely to outline the approach and how it might provide a framework for the physical education programme and, thus, for a central core for the wider games experience. It would appear that there is a measure of agreement that teaching for understanding has allowed a refocusing of games teaching in a number of ways, some quite unexpected. Teachers have made the point that mixed-sex teaching is easier with a teaching for understanding approach, but in itself this does not necessarily ensure equal opportunity (girls in mixed-sex lessons taught with 'understanding' had only 12% to 34% of possession in invasion games [Turvey & Laws, 1988]).

The approach designed to allow children with all abilities to take part in games does of course allow those with disabilities to be included. It follows that an approach that allows those with special needs, including the very talented, to be embraced in the lesson is particularly valuable. The fact that physical education might demand the input of additional specialist help to meet the needs of these children raises some interesting possibilities.

Why the Need to Rethink Games?

It is important to note that the approach was not developed solely to make games more available to the less able. In 1982 Bunker and Thorpe made the following comments:

> Observation of present games teaching shows at best, a series of highly structured lessons leaning heavily on the teaching of techniques, or at worst lessons which rely on the children themselves to sustain interest in the game. This paper is based on the opinion that these approaches have led to:
>
> a)   a large percentage of children achieving little success due to the emphasis on performance, i.e. 'doing'
>
> b)   the majority of school leavers 'knowing' very little about games
>
> c)   the production of supposedly 'skilful' players who in fact possess inflexible techniques and poor decision making capacity
>
> d)   the development of teacher/coach dependent performers
>
> e)   the failure to develop 'thinking' spectators and 'knowing' administrators at a time when games (and sport) are an important form of entertainment in the leisure industry. (p. 9)

A model was proposed that asked that the teacher reverse the traditional order of teaching games by placing the game and tactics centrally in the physical education lesson rather than leaving them for the extracurricular team practice. Isolated skill development is advocated only when the need for such is recognized by the child. The vast majority of skill practice would take place outside the lesson if the children were motivated.

The steps in the model clearly show this progression.

1. *Game*—A game is needed that recognizes the ability of the child.

2. *Game appreciation*—The authors felt that teachers always made too many assumptions about a child's ability to recognize the purpose of a game and that time should be given for the children to see what the game was all about. If rules were included, as has been found to be necessary, the appreciation of the game would be greater. The children, in understanding why rules are necessary, might appreciate the necessity to accept rules for a 'good' game.

3. *Tactical awareness*—The authors felt that children would enjoy solving the problems posed by the game and would thus gain the knowledge necessary to understand the games they might play or watch.

4. *Decision making: What to do and how to do it*—It was felt necessary to divide these two phases. Two children might well know that it would be wise to play a slow drop shot in badminton (the what to do), but one child with limited skill might play the shot with a simple push, whereas another, more gifted and aware of the need for disguise, might well concentrate on a late wrist check. This leads to the next step.

5. *Skill execution*—This is always assessed as individually appropriate. For example the pushed drop shot just described might be entirely appropriate when the state of the game and the ability of the performer are considered.

6. *Performance*—Teachers can still be aware of the absolute performance levels for assessment. The teacher can still recognize that the pushed drop shot is not as good in absolute terms as the disguised drop. Yet, this absolute measure will be insignificant within the learning situation.

Any assessment in games should thus include game appreciation, tactical awareness, the making of appropriate decisions, and appropriate skill execution as well as, or even instead of, performance. In addition, assessment should of course satisfy the broader aims of enhancing the learning process, providing feedback, and giving evidence of achievement.

To convince teachers that this was a viable alternative, courses were always done practically, but it was necessary to revise some traditional assumptions. For years there had been a general acceptance that a games lesson began with a warm-up, had a skill phase and, if the children were well behaved, might end with a game. The possible historical reasons for this lesson plan and the focus on technique has been laid firmly at the door of those training teachers and coaches (Thorpe & Bunker, 1983).

The model can provide guidelines for the games teacher or coach, from primary teacher to international coach. Many nonspecialist primary teachers accept the logic of using the intrinsic interest in the game to promote knowledge; yet, at the opposite extreme, Whitaker (personal communication, 1988) uses this approach with international hockey players. Greenwood (1986), in his book *Think Rugby*, stresses the importance of good decision making, and it is interesting to note that a major section of his book is entitled 'The Quest for Space', a central theme in many of the units presented in the understanding approach.

Throughout the 1980s a number of examples of games units based on the understanding approach have been included in either the *Bulletin of Physical Education* or the *British Journal of Physical Education*, and several are included in *Physical Education: Recent Curriculum Developments* (School Curriculum Development Committee, 1988). If one places an understanding of games to the fore, one starts to consider which games are best in providing the knowledge base. The games that illustrate a point clearly may bear little resemblance to the games we witness on television or in the park (particularly in the early years), but equally there is a need to investigate this recognizable game or sport at some stage. The natural outcome of a teaching for understanding approach is the development of a games education that ensures that children experience and gain insight into the wide variety of games possible.

A Games Education

Once one seeks the underlying principles of games to aid understanding, it becomes apparent that certain games have many things in common. The principles that pertain to soccer are very similar to those that pertain to hockey. There are some important differences, but these become clearer when set against the basic, common conceptual framework of the games. It follows, therefore, that games can be classified according to their different tactical demands. A number of classification systems have been studied (Almond, 1986).

Fundamentals for Developing a Games Curriculum

The use of game classification systems allows a more appropriate sampling of games. It has to be recognized that to understand an invasion team game (like hockey) might take longer than understanding a singles divided-court game (like badminton). It therefore follows that a little more time might be allocated to team invasion games, but there is considerable evidence that the balance has usually already been heavily weighted toward this form of game. *Sampling* becomes a major factor in the design of the games curriculum. Once this fundamental is accepted, there is no need to offer every game.

If one considers that the understanding approach directs attention to the development of knowledge, some attention should be given to the complexity of the game type offered. In fact, it is not unusual for the most tactically complex games (large-side invasion games) to be offered first to the primary child. Is this sound education? A second fundamental that guides the order of the games curriculum is *tactical complexity*.

Finally, because adult games are rarely appropriate for youngsters, some form of modification is necessary. If the intention is to provide a game that is as like the adult game as possible (e.g. short tennis and other mini-games), then this modification is for *representation*. If a game is modified dramatically to accentuate a point then this is *modification by exaggeration* (e.g. playing badminton on long, thin courts to accentuate the long/short nature of the play). The use of these four fundamentals in developing a games curriculum for the 5- to 16-year-old has been illustrated elsewhere (Thorpe & Bunker, 1989; Thorpe, Bunker, & Almond, 1984).

If it is accepted that all children should be allowed to wrestle with the problems posed by particular sorts of games, then inevitably some of the traditional assumptions made about games for boys and games for girls will be eroded. I would like to think that all children would have a chance to use the relatively simple skill of running with the ball or passing to a teammate in an attempt to get the ball over the opponent's line. Equally, all children would play divided court games at various stages of their education. In the 'feeder' primary school, with only a playground, this might involve a form of one-on-one throw volleyball/tennis. In the secondary school, with a large sports hall, a half-court badminton game might be offered. The concepts are reinforced as the game moves toward a recognizable sport. The movement toward the recognizable game prepares all children to step into the outside world.

Competition is inherent in games; we play against opponents and try to score. If we accept that many children seem to play sport to be with friends and 'just' to be active, though, then we might change the way we present competitive options. The children who play hard and fail to keep score are telling the teacher something. In small-side or individual games, the option of whether to join a competitive league of similar players or to continue to play and practise with a partner can be easily built into a lesson. Time spent equally with the children who choose competition and the children who do not can do much to show the group that you are interested in activity and development rather than just competition and excellence. I see few teachers presenting this form of choice to children: The class will be either competitive or not at any moment of time. It might be that the physical education teacher sees the development of appropriate responses toward winning and losing as important; the fact that game results are always relative to the opponent can do much to show how many sports rely on a co-operative agreement to meet on near-equal terms to play the game. 'It is easy to win. Play someone who is clearly below your ability!'

What of Skill and Performance?

To be a good performer at most sports requires considerable practice. The limited curriculum time and the mixed-ability class of 30 does not, and perhaps never has, produced high-level performers. Those of us who have played games all our lives know that most skill practice occurs away from the physical education lesson, at play, during the game, or even in contemplation before and after the event. It is for this reason that a number of individuals have questioned the traditional approach that one must be formally taught the skills of the game if one is to play. It might be that the games lessons concentration on skill (*technique* might be a better word in that the skill was taken out of context) grew out of the traditional desire to make children more skilful. Teaching for understanding has always placed technique development in the context of the game at the level of the child. Certainly the teacher can help with technique, but caution should be exercised. Does the player need it? Is he or she ready to receive it? Can it be delivered in a way that will ensure that it transfers back into the game?

It may be that approaches of this sort, linking so strongly the learning of the response to the context of a game, produce a different form of learning. Read

(1988), in distinguishing between technical competence and practical knowledge and by showing the many ways in which the nature of responses are determined by their game contexts, questions again the wisdom of isolated technical practice.

In part, the development of teaching for understanding was a reaction to watching some children fail to learn a given skill year after year whilst other children practised this very same skill, which they had mastered several years before. As such, the approach questions the basic premise that skill development is the primary aim in the games lesson. It might be in enhancing intrinsic motivation toward the game, playing more appropriate games, or practising skills that have a clear relevance to the learner (rather than the teacher) in the game context that the player becomes a more skilful performer. The teacher who can identify that one (or a few pupils) would welcome more intensive technical work should have a range of strategies available, such as teaching styles that allow children to work alone or with a partner within the lesson, lunch-time practice sessions, contacts with out-of-school clubs and coaches, ensuring that these needs are met.

The PEA (1987) reported that teachers stated that the learning of motor skills and physical development are the primary aims of the physical education teacher. In games it might be that this aim is best met by placing attention away from the skill!

Summary

Games in the Curriculum and Beyond

The National Curriculum might accelerate the movement toward a more logical games education. There seems to be considerable evidence that the games programmes offered to date are poorly balanced and consist of a series of discrete games presented in no logical order. The games curriculum as outlined might aim to accomplish the following:

- To produce children who have insights into all games because they have experienced samples of the different types of games
- To produce children who are skilful at games in that they make appropriate responses (relative to their own abilities) to the particular problems posed by the games
- To produce children who understand the experience of competing and also that games can be played with different degrees of competitiveness
- To help children understand the dynamics of team efficiency
- To produce children who enjoy playing games and feel confident to play games outside the curriculum time
- To produce children who know how to modify games to make them work, know how to practise, and know how to prepare for a match; that is, they are involved in and responsible for their own learning but are equally able to cooperate with others to play games

- To produce children who understand the benefits (and debits) that can be gained by playing games
- To produce some children who wish to operate as leaders, coaches, administrators and so forth

If all this happens, some children will be achieving excellence.

Proposals

To provide a full and interesting games experience for our children, it will be necessary to give far more realistic guidance to the primary teacher. Rather than see the presence of qualified others as a threat in the games lesson, this author believes that by their relieving some of the major pressure of organizational control from the teacher, more education could occur.

At the secondary level there is a need to identify the games education that all children should receive, further, the physical education teacher has to consider how children can extend this experience outside the curriculum. It may not be helpful to separate school-based sport from outside-school sport, in that this can produce replication. Rather, the physical education teacher of the future should look to ways of supporting sport outside school and bringing appropriately trained individuals into the school.

The National Curriculum may give the impetus to a far more logical games education. The major reports into school sport lead us toward a more coordinated provision of the games experience outside the curriculum. The two go hand in hand. There are many teachers prepared to work hard to produce a good games experience, and this at a time when the physical education profession seems to have identified, in the British Council of Physical Education, a focal point for discussion and action. The stage is set.

References

Alderman, R.B., & Wood, N.L. (1976). An analysis of incentive motivation in Canadian athletics. *Canadian Journal of Applied Sports Sciences,* 1, 169-176.

Almond, L. (1986). Reflecting on themes: A games classification. In R.D. Thorpe (Ed.), *Rethinking games teaching* (pp. 71-72). Loughborough: Loughborough University.

Almond, L. (1989). The place of physical education in the curriculum. In L. Almond (Ed.), *The place of physical education in schools* (pp. 13-36). London: Kogan Page.

Almond, L., & Thorpe, R.D. (1988). Asking teachers to research. *Journal of Teaching in Physical Education,* 7, 221-227.

Association of County Councils. (1988). In R.D. Thorpe (Ed.), *Sports leadership: A consultation exercise.* Unpublished report, Sports Council, London.

Association of Metropolitan Authorities. (1988). In R.D. Thorpe (Ed.), *Sports Leadership: A consultation exercise.* Unpublished report, Sports Council, London.

Biddle, S.J.H. (1986). Incentive schemes in exercise: Saints or sinners? *Health & Physical Education Project Newsletter, 3*, 4-7.

Bunker, D.J., & Thorpe, R.D. (1982). A model for the teaching of games in the secondary schools. *Bulletin of Physical Education, 10*, 9-16.

Campbell, S. (1986). What can sport offer children? *Sports Teacher, 5*, 2.

Campbell, S. (1988). Initial teacher training: Meeting the demands. The sport lobby. In *Conference Proceedings of the Standing Conference on Physical Education in Teacher Education* (pp. 20-23). Loughborough Standing Conference on Physical Education in Teacher Education.

Chappel, R. (1989). School sport in Great Britain. *Bulletin of Physical Education, 23*, 152-153.

Coaching Association of Canada. (1972). *National Coaching Certification Program: Coaching theory 2.* Ottawa: Author.

Cockerill, S.A., & Hardy, C.A. (1989). Problems of extra-curricular provision in physical education. *Bulletin of Physical Education, 24*, 28-32.

Coventry teachers. (1986). *Coventry teachers explore teaching for understanding.* Coventry: Local Education Authority.

Csikszentmihalyi, M. (1975). *Beyond boredom and anxiety.* San Francisco: Jossey-Bass.

Dickenson, B.F., & Sparkes, A.C. (1988). Pupil definitions of physical education. *British Journal of Physical Education, 2*(Research Supplement), 6-7.

English Schools Football Association. (1988). *Report on: The effect of the teachers contract on association football in schools.* London: Author.

Graham, I. (1971). *Teaching tennis in schools.* Unpublished dissertation, Loughborough University, Loughborough.

Greenwood, J.T. (1986). *Think rugby: A guide to purposeful team play.* London: A & C Blake.

Inner London Education Authority. (1988). *My favourite subject: Report of the Working Party on Physical Education and School Sports.* London: Author.

Lawton, J. (1987). *A comparison of two teaching methods.* Unpublished master's thesis, Loughborough University, Loughborough.

Murdoch, E. (1987). *Sport in schools.* Desk study commissioned by the Department of Education and Science and the Department of the Environment. London: Department of Education and Science and Department of the Environment.

Physical Education Association. (1987). *Physical education in schools.* London: Ling.

Pigott, R.E. (1982). A psychological basis for new trends in games teaching. *Bulletin of Physical Education, 19*, 17-22.

Read, B.R. (1988). Practical knowledge and the teaching of games. In *Essays in physical education, recreation management and sports science* (pp. 111-122). Loughborough: Loughborough University.

School Curriculum Development Committee. (1988). *Physical education: Recent curriculum developments.* London: National Curriculum Committee.

School Sport Forum. (1988). Sport and young people. London: Sports Council.

Smith, J. (1980). In *Sport in the community: The next 10 years.* London: Sports Council.

Thomas, P. (1988). Initial teacher training: Meeting the demands: Perceptions from the schools. In *Conference Proceedings of the Standing Conference on Physical Education in Teacher Education* (pp. 7-9). Loughborough Standing Conference on Physical Education in Teacher Education.

Thorpe, R.D. (1988). *Sports leadership: A consultation exercise*. Unpublished report, Sports Council.

Thorpe, R.D. (in press). *Meeting the needs of the 5-16 year old*. Conference report, Cheshire Teachers Conference, Blackpool.

Thorpe, R.D., & Bunker, D.J. (1983). A new approach to the teaching of games in the physical education curriculum. In *Teaching team sports: AIESEP [Association Internationale des Superieures d' Education Physique] Congress proceedings* (pp. 229-238). Rome: Comitato Olimpico Nazionale Italiano [CONI].

Thorpe, R.D., & Bunker, D.J. (1989). A changing focus in games education. In L. Almond (Ed.), *The place of physical education in schools* (pp. 42-71). London: Kogan Page.

Thorpe, R.D., Bunker, D.J., & Almond, L. (1984). A change in focus for the teaching of games. In M. Piéron & G. Graham (Eds.), *The 1984 Olympic Scientific Congress Proceedings: Vol. 6. Sport Pedagogy* (pp. 163-169). Champaign, IL: Human Kinetics.

Thorpe, R.D., Bunker, D.J., & Almond, L. (1986). *Rethinking games teaching*. Loughborough: Loughborough University.

Turvey, J., & Laws, C. (1988). Are girls losing out? The effects of mixed-sex grouping on girls performance in physical education. *British Journal of Physical Education*, **19**, 253-255.

Wade, A. (1967). *The F.A. guide to training and coaching*. London: Heinemann.

Weinberg, R.S. (1984). The relationship between extrinsic rewards and intrinsic motivation in sport. In J.M. Silva & R.S. Weinberg (Eds.), *Psychological foundations of sport* (pp. 177-187). Champaign, IL: Human Kinetics.

Whitehead, J. (1988). Encouraging participation by understanding more about motivation. In *Proceedings of the Annual Conference of the Northern Ireland Institute of Coaching* (pp. 13-22). Belfast: Northern Ireland Institute of Coaching.

Williams, A. (in press). Changes in provision of PGCE courses and the effects on teaching of P.E. in primary and secondary schools. In *Proceedings of the British Universities Physical Education Association Conference*. Loughborough: Loughborough University.

Williams, A. & Jenkins, C. (1988). A curriculum for a fit state? The National Curriculum proposals and physical education. *British Journal of Physical Education*, **19**, 112-115.

Chapter 6

Equal Opportunities and Physical Education

Margaret Talbot

Equality of opportunity, on the face of it, seems like an unquestionable educational aim. And yet, when one begins to examine it, one quickly realizes that it can be a minefield of value-loaded and emotive rhetoric and that what is needed above all is clarification between *concept* and *intent*, the setting of achievable objectives, and the recognition that strategies to achieve aims and objectives are just that, not ends in themselves. Further, it is important to recognize and acknowledge that there *will* be disagreements about the appropriateness or effectiveness of specific strategies but that such disagreement does not remove the validity or integrity of the intentions behind them.

Attempting to establish parity in a social world of inequality is not a simple task. It has to be recognized that in the process of equalizing, there will be people who perceive changes inevitably as losses, if for no other reason than that they fear change or because they fear the loss of status or power that they associate with moves towards parity. In the same social world, there will be people who could be assessed as 'suffering' from inequality but who themselves do not perceive their status to be a problem—because their self-concepts and self-esteem have been formed from their ability to make sense of and to value their social positions on terms which they may feel are unchangeable and immutable, or because they feel they would lose more by challenging their self-concepts than by continuing to live by them. To attack these social positions is to undermine the bases of people's ability to make sense of, and construct dignity in, their lives.

This is *not* an argument for maintaining the status quo. It is a warning that any social change is a complex process, involving the balancing of the ethics and effects of different strategies. To understand the fears of others is to know better how to allay them. But if education is to be anything more than a predictable channeling process, then presuppositions must be confronted and examined, not necessarily so that everyone is brought to agree with each other but so that issues can be recognized, their implications discussed, and their effects on the limitation of potential recognized.

The notion of equality is central to much educational and social policy. In physical education and sports education, we reconcile the contradiction inherent between the intrinsically competitive, exclusively rewarding nature of many of our activities and the ideal of equality. We use the argument that the process of physical education is based on the intention to promote the exploration of individual potential and that all children are given equal opportunity to participate at their own levels. However, in the various interpretations of equality, there is a complex hidden agenda that significantly affects the way in which physical education or sports programmes might be delivered but that is hardly ever explicit and seldom explored (see Talbot, 1988).

Most of my arguments in this chapter are based on issues and strategies in gender inequalities, but I believe that to begin to understand the dynamics of any one area of inequality is to begin to understand others.

Equal Treatment

When challenged regarding their practice of equality, many physical educationists would argue, very strongly, that they always treat children equally. Often they extend this contention to their relationships with colleagues and other professionals. On the face of it, this is a convincing case: What could be 'fairer' than treating everyone the same, offering the same programme? But there are two central flaws in this model that make it unacceptable as a central element in the process of achieving equality of opportunity.

First, the principle of equal treatment tends to ignore the fact that people differ in their capacities, interests, resources and previous experience. To treat them identically would be to ignore their individuality and limit the extent to which we might draw on their various backgrounds, interests and abilities. Second, equal treatment is simply not possible in practice. No good teacher treats all the children in a mixed-ability class the same. Classroom interaction studies show that teachers consistently give more attention to boys than to girls in coeducational settings, that their judgements differ when the same behaviour displayed by boys is displayed by girls, and that interaction is similarly affected by factors of ethnicity, social class and age. Even when teachers are made aware of this, first they refuse to believe it, and then, when convinced that they are indeed behaving inequitably, they find it very difficult to change; even teachers who are committed to equal opportunities face real and powerful habit unraveling! The equal treatment principle also ignores the pervasiveness and the power of our differential expectations of girls and boys, women and men. Recent research indicates that the same is true for expectations of children from different racial and ethnic groups and social classes.

Another pertinent question to beg when met with claims of equal or the same treatment is 'The same as what?' The nature of the sameness of the treatment is itself open to examination, question and redefinition. What is the benchmark being used? In a *Sunday Times* article ('Girls Measure Up', 1989) about girls being accepted into boys' public school sixth forms, the title ('Girls measure up to challenge') gives us an immediate insight into the norm being used, apparently without question, in these schools. It is also worth recording that all the stated educational benefits gained from girls being in public school sixth forms accrue to either the schools (from fees, social mix etc.) or to the boys (civilizing influence, social mix, better learning atmosphere); no clear benefit for the girls was apparent, except of course the honour of 'measuring up'! It is unfortunate that the General Secretary of the Physical Education Association seemed to be in danger of the same error when arguing that mixed physical education might even help prevent soccer hooliganism. He wrote, 'Do we, as a profession, contribute, even in some small measure, to the "macho" part of the description (of soccer fans) by continuing to divide boys and girls for physical education in most mixed secondary schools?' But he redeemed himself by showing that he was aware of some of the dangers when he wrote, 'Or is there enough evidence to demonstrate that girls are being deprived of equal opportunity of access to sport *because* of mixed physical education and should not be sacrificed to the need to "gentle" macho males?' (Gibbon, 1988, p. 147).

Teacher interaction with colleagues and pupils reveals a great deal about the values and beliefs of that teacher. The kind of person that teacher is also affects the pupils' construction of norms of behaviour and parity of treatment.

One may add philosophical respectability to the 'treat them all the same' notion of equality: R.S. Peters (1966) put forward a presumptive principle of equality:

It does not prescribe positively that all human beings be treated alike; it is a presumption against treating them differently, in any respect, until grounds for distinction have been shewn. . . . The onus of justification rests on whoever would make distinctions. (p. 121)

Again, this principle is attractive until one tries to apply it. The crucial question here is 'Different from what?' Who decides what is the norm against which people should be judged, and how is the norm ever changed? The suspicion of a tendency to establish absolute standards through such a principle immediately undermines it.

So the 'treat them all the same' claim is both inoperable in practice and unequal in its effects, even though it can be a powerful tool in *questioning* the basis of unequal treatment when related implicitly to category, whether gender, ethnicity, sexuality or age.

Equal Outcomes

Another interpretation of equality is that of equal outcomes; instead of advocating equal treatment regardless of individual differences, it accommodates these differences in order to work towards equality of outcome. The problem with this approach is that it chooses to override untapped potential in the concern with the objective of the outcome of sameness; it thus cannot be accepted as an overarching educational strategy. A common and valid criticism of this principle is that in practice it would reduce performance to the lowest common denominator. Clearly, there are times when teachers try to control the differences between children within the same teaching group in order to encourage progress among the less confident or the less able, to share out participation and involvement, to encourage the more able to consider the needs of others, or even to enlist the help of the more able in mentoring or teaching others. But teachers rarely deny these differences in absolute terms; rather, they try to value the different contributions of different children. Good teachers also try to bring children to realize and respect other people's differences. Equality of outcome is particularly problematic to apply because it is impossible to determine at what point the end product of equality is achieved.

Egalitarianism

A popular interpretation of equality is that of shared humanity, or egalitarianism, a principle forming the basis of the constitutions of many countries. The argument runs that we are all human beings, with the same human rights, so we therefore should not suffer from any form of discrimination. In this sense, it is a useful notion for encouraging children to express themselves and to learn to value others' differences and for discouraging them from mistreating other people merely because of the category to which they belong. It is a challenge to the denial of the essential humanity of members of ethnic minorities, women and girls, old people, gay people, disabled people. The film *One Flew Over the Cuckoo's Nest* was so shocking precisely because it demonstrated the denial of a mental patient's essential humanity.

This interpretation also has utility because it forms a basis for law: Most countries now have legislation that forbids discrimination of treatment on the basis of membership of categories like race and sex. It is thus a negative interpretation of equality; it tells us what not to do but fails to help us decide how we should behave toward different people in an unequal society. This interpretation gives us a kind of 'baseline' guidance for behaviour, beneath which we are aware we may be sanctioned or punished for our actions. However, this interpretation does not necessarily change our attitudes, although it may, if we allow it, provide us with an opportunity to confront our own presuppositions and prejudices and to examine critically the ways in which our professional institutions may informally or formally discriminate against certain categories of people.

This interpretation also gives us a firm foundation for refuting or challenging justifications of inequality as 'natural'. I was quite shocked to read, for example, in the 1988 Alberta Physical Education Curriculum's section on coeducational physical education, that among the inherent capability differences between boys and girls is included rhythm! This kind of assumption is dangerous and deterministic and must be challenged. Where more clearly physiological differences are the subject of discussion, the guide points out the importance of the overlap between boys and girls and the misleading nature of averages. Yet even here it still provides dangerous generalizations such as the following, with no qualifications related to age, ethnic differences or levels of training: 'Boys have more strength, height, weight and cardiorespiratory endurance than girls', and 'Girls generally possess greater flexibility, rhythmic ability and buoyancy' (p. 13).

Without even questioning the inevitability of these qualities, the report goes on to recommend separate standards for boys and girls 'where *any combination* [my emphasis] of strength, endurance, height, weight, lean body mass, flexibility, buoyancy or rhythm contribute to the evaluation of physical performance' (p. 13). In any class of 13-year-old boys and girls, it might be difficult to attribute differences of, for example, height and endurance exclusively to gender, yet this is precisely what the report is suggesting should be done, so reifying and perpetuating differences in expectation.

The curriculum guide is clearly well intended, but in this particular area it shows confusion and a lack of relevant information. Although it gives guidance on modes of teacher behaviour that should be avoided if equality is to be taken seriously, it ignores much of the research data available on coeducational and single-sex groupings. The same criticism could be made of a great deal of mixed work that is being done or experimented with in this country. In secondary schools, falling school rolls, difficulties in replacing physical education staff and sometimes a feeling among physical education staff that it is 'right' to end the 'apartheid' that has existed for so long between boys' and girls' physical education have accelerated the impetus to move from single-sex to coeducational provision in physical education. Mixed groupings, however, do not guarantee improvements in either parity or equality of opportunity.

Equal Opportunity

Returning to interpretations of equality, the most frequently used principle of equality, especially in contemporary British education, is the principle of equality of opportunity. The problem inherent in this principle is that it depends heavily on the notion of making education equally *accessible* to all. The idea of widening educational franchise by offering access presumes that if all structural and social constraints can be controlled or removed, people then have equal opportunity to compete both through and within the educational system. In this sense, people are not actively prevented from taking part in education or physical education. The problem in applying this argument is that access is not the same as opportunity. Similarly, equity is not the same as equality of opportunity.

> Equality of opportunity should not be reduced to equality of coercion. Nor need it be. It is not synonymous with equality of material resources for the education of each person. It is a more complex form of personal liberty because it deals not with equal agents, but genetically differentiated individuals. . . .
>
> . . . opportunity can be understood as a specific case of individual freedom. (Green, 1988, pp. 3-4)

The distinction between access and opportunity is based on two forms of freedom: freedom *from* constraint confers access, whereas freedom *to* do as one wishes confers opportunity. This active and positive criterion of opportunity is crucial because it reveals the significance of both the perception of the individual concerned and the obligation on the part of the educational provider to evaluate and seek to understand the nature of the structural and hidden aspects of the curriculum that affect that individual perception.

For example, we may feel, as physical educationists, that we have provided equality of opportunity for children of primary school age to take part in programmes of physical activity because the same programme is presented to all children, regardless of category membership. According to Walker (1988), 'In choosing groups and exercising options people are not equal. It would seem important for school counsellors to add a recognition of this to their appreciation of the issues' (p. 15). Ann Hall (1987), too, has pointed out that it is simply unrealistic and naive to ignore the strength and power of the surrounding and preceding sport culture. Yet, an uncritical move to coeducational physical education does just that. It ignores children's previous cultural experience, resulting in less than equal experiences for girls and boys in coeducational physical education.

Equal *access* may, indeed, be the case: no one is prevented by virtue of sex, religion or other category membership from entering the programme (although in reality in physical education, this does continue to be the case). But so often with this kind of model, the relevance of the sex of the teacher, the preconditions for access and associated expectations, the choice of activities offered, the interactions within coeducational classes and the previous experience and relative skill levels of the children are not seen as central. When members of certain groups fail to gain access or perform badly having gained access, they may be said to be 'wasting opportunities'; rarely is consideration given to the ways in which the form or delivery of the provision is itself exclusive, at least in the perception of those who feel that participation is impossible or even irrelevant. The tendency then is to adopt a pathological approach and 'to blame the victim', labeling whole categories pejoratively by their nonparticipation: 'Boys won't dance.' 'Girls don't like contact sports.'

Myths

These labels rapidly assume the status of myths, which may or may not depend on generalizable observations but which are notoriously difficult to challenge or disprove. One common myth is that older adolescent girls dislike vigorous physical activity, but have you ever watched the same girls at a disco? The point here is that those who promulgate the myth have failed to take into account the perceptions of the girls themselves. Further, such promulgators have excluded from their own perceptions evidence that clearly contradicts the generalization they are making. Janice Butcher (1983) has observed that personal attribute studies have been unhelpful in explaining why girls do or do not take part in physical activity, which underlines the limitations of any theory that seeks to explain non-participation in terms of the nonparticipant rather than in terms of the activity or the nature of its delivery.

Coeducation—Equality of Opportunity?

The distinction between access and opportunity is crucial to questioning the assumption that coeducational physical education confers equal opportunities. Boys and girls may in some schools have equal rights of *access* to physical education, but do they also have equal *opportunities* to learn and to express themselves through and in physical activity? How *is* the agenda set in coeducational physical education? In spite of this, there currently seems to be a prevailing assumption that coeducation implicitly confers equality of opportunity. Physical education teachers who see themselves as radical, progressive and committed to the promotion of equal opportunities routinely brush aside the caution of those who seek to maintain the strengths of single-sex traditions in physical education. Strengths there are, and I believe that we are in danger of both ignoring and losing them. This co-educationalist single-mindedness may be understandable when you take into account the propensity of the 'major games dinosaurs' to promulgate the need to keep single-sex provision on grounds more related to identification with school team traditions than with a concern for the efficient and relevant delivery of curriculum physical education. This polarization is unfortunate, stemming in part from our failure as a profession either to distinguish clearly between curriculum physical education and school sport or to distinguish between single-sex grouping and single-sex teaching. The debate is clearly illustrated in some of the papers in John Evans's (1988) recent book (see, for example, Evans and Clarke, 1988, Evans and Davies, 1988).

There are three main flaws in the assumption that coeducation implicitly confers equality of opportunity; these will be discussed next.

Detraction From Girls' Educational Performances

First, there is overwhelming evidence that coeducation detracts from girls' educational performances. Generally, the findings (from physical education and other subjects), apart from the data on teacher interaction that I have already mentioned, show the following:

- Girls are less actively involved in coeducational than in single-sex settings.
- Boys actively harass and limit girls' behaviour, often ridiculing their efforts.
- Girls perform less well in coeducational than single-sex settings.
- Girls' and boys' behaviour and role play are more polarized and more opposed in coeducational than in single-sex settings.
- Boys dominate leadership roles, and girls take on subservient ones, in coeducational settings—they revert to stereotype.
- In coeducational schools, subject choice is more sex-stereotyped (boys take science, girls take arts) than in single-sex schools.

It is interesting that, where single-sex mathematics classes have been held in coeducational schools, the girls' performance has significantly improved (whereas in coeducational groups they consistently underperformed) and the boys' performance has deteriorated. Even more interesting was the teachers' perception that this was problematic: Boys should not be put in a situation where they became disadvantaged. Thus, it is clear that boys can gain a great deal more from coeducation than girls do, such as better levels of discipline and a greater share of teachers' attention. These findings are borne out in the context of physical education by research carried out, for example, by Sheila Scraton (1990), Julie Turvey and Chris Laws (1988), John Evans et al. (1987), Raymond Dunbar and Mary O'Sullivan (1986) and John Evans (1989). As John Evans and Gill Clarke (1988) remark,

> Despite the not insignificant and paradigmatic changes in content and organization which had been effected by these teachers, there was very little pedagogical change of a kind which would challenge or change the authority relationships of the classroom or confront or alter the typical gendered attitudes and behaviours of children or indeed of the teachers. (p. 138)

Unquestioned Norms

The second flaw (or danger) is that the move to coeducation implies a kind of female 'catch-up' or 'measure up' to males, an assumption that male standards are always those to which we should all aspire. Maybe this sounds self-evident. But in Britain, it was *women* who began the profession of physical education in the 1880s and 1890s; and men did not begin training as physical education specialists until 1933. As Sheila Fletcher (1984) so ably describes, it was 'women first'. Therefore, we evolved a tradition of single-sex physical education training and programmes, with established quality, innovation and range within the female physical education tradition. Arguably, girls in British single-sex physical education have a wider range of physical activities than boys, and they often have better access to school facilities, especially during bad weather. Our Sex Discrimination Act allows sex differentiation but not discrimination; this is a grey area of distinction, and the legal position is changing, in some cases due more to European law than to British legislation. But the established female physical education tradition does mean that we can be more critical and powerful in our negotiation of a common or coeducational physical education programme than can our counterparts in North America.

Lack of Questioning and Self-Criticism

The third flaw lies in the conventional response in physical education and sports provision to the observation that fewer girls than boys take part in physical activity. Often, ways are proposed to encourage more girls to take part in existing programmes, or programmes may be adapted in a stereotypical way. Our failure as professionals here is that we have neglected to evaluate the effects of our own practices and procedures, an element that we persuade our student teachers is essential in the curriculum process. Sheila Scraton (1990), in confirming this assessment, refers to the 'ad hoc basis of much of the educational innovation in this area', a finding that replicates that of Evans et al. (1987).

Achieving Equality of Opportunity

Working towards equality of opportunity in physical education and sports education is not merely the removal of structural constraint. It involves the understanding and appreciation of pupils' responses to ideologies of masculinity and femininity and the way these relate for them to physical education. Working towards equality also requires critical review of our own work; rigorous and continuous appraisal of our professional institutions and practices; honest analysis of the relationships between different groups within the profession; and challenging instances of sexism, racism and homophobia.

In this way, we might begin to address some of the issues that are at the heart of the educational aim of equality of opportunity. For example, for whom is equality of opportunity desired? Is this intention limited to all the children we teach, or only some of them, or do we also apply it to ourselves and our fellow professionals? Would equality in professional terms relate only to individuals, or also to the aspects of the subject area they teach, coach or research? Does it also pervade all levels of delivery, from the elementary school to postgraduate or postdoctoral research? How is the equality judged, and by whom? Do we each take responsibility for this? Or do we 'pass the buck' to others, even to members of the very groups who suffer most from the inequalities? After all, we may reason, it's their problem, not mine!

If we do take on part of a collective responsibility, what are the categories of people who we feel are not enjoying equality of opportunity now, and what are the reasons for this? How do we define inequality, and how do we arrive at the standard or norm by which we would wish to redress the balance? Crudely speaking, if we are trying to 'measure up', what is the unit of measurement, and whose achievements provide the reference points that define deficiency or superiority?

Three Stages of Problem Solving

William Solesbury (1976) has suggested that any problem must pass through three distinct stages before it can be successfully resolved. First, the problem must command *attention*; it must become visible. The Physical Education Association (PEA) recently convened a one-day conference where various advisers and inspectors addressed the issue through in-service courses and conferences. However, mere visibility is not sufficient. If the issue becomes marginalized or ghettoized as any one group's problem rather than one shared by the whole profession, dialogue becomes stereotyped and restricted. This cannot substitute for public, concerned discussion of the issues involved; tokenism is not acceptable.

Second, the problem must claim *legitimacy*. Issues of equity must be seen as significant and important by people in power, who need to possess the attitudes and empathy to re-frame our profession to make it more effective in the classroom, and more accessible to those who traditionally have been excluded, trivialized or marginalized. Awareness achieves nothing without commitment on the part of *all* the people who influence events.

> This will require more than awareness, of course. It will require creative intervention in the youth cultures of pupils, concentrating on those cultural modes, such as sport and music, where the actual dynamics of cultural hier-archies are played out at their strongest. Teachers will need to discover, in the first instance, points at which changes in intercultural articulation could work to the *mutual* advantage of, for example, oppressing and oppressed groups. (Walker, 1988, p. 16)

Once such a happy state of affairs has been reached, the third stage of *invoking action* can be entered. But the nature and efficacy of action depends so much on the quality of the enquiry and the information acquired during the previous two stages. It also has to be asked whether action can be sufficiently radical or sensitive to achieve real change.

Dimensions of Change

Andrew Sparkes (1987) has argued that attempts to introduce innovations in schools have had a limited effect in producing change at the classroom level. He points out the inevitability of failure when, for instance, introducing mixed-ability grouping without corresponding change to mixed-ability teaching. The same distinction can be applied to coeducational grouping and teaching. Sparkes identifies the following three dimensions of change:

- Use of new or revised materials
- Use of new skills, teaching approaches, styles and strategies, i.e. teaching practices
- Changes in beliefs, attitudes, values, ideologies and understanding, with reference to pedagogical assumptions and theories

The first of these, new materials, is easy, and physical education has been quick to add new activities to the programme, including some which were claimed to avoid sex bias (remember Tchouk Ball?). With the second, new skills and practices, we have had mixed results but some progress. But how far have we progressed with the third, changes in beliefs and values? I would argue that, with regard to equality, this should not be the third but the first stage; certainly equal-opportunities work in education has proceeded with this strategy. Sparkes (1987) also points out that 'if we are to talk of *real* change as opposed to superficial change then we must view innovation as multidimensional and as a process—not a product' (p. 4).

It is therefore important for us all to remember that equality is a long-term, pervasive issue and cannot be 'blitzed'. Focused programmes are still only a small step in a long process of changing entrenched attitudes. Strategies need to be long term, continuous and monitored.

Nature of Professionalism

Another element on which we must seek clarification, before we begin to answer some of these questions, is the nature of professionalism and its role in perpetuating unquestioned absolutes and norms in physical education. Professions are said to be more than occupations: They are not only important means of passing on technical information but are also vehicles for the expression of social values and interests.

> In a very real sense, professions are the guardians of public values. If they are perceived to be exercising this responsibility in a partisan fashion, the question . . . 'Who is to guard the guards themselves?' . . . will become the central one. . . . In a liberal democracy, self-control . . . is to be preferred to central or bureaucratic control. It is for this reason that systematic attention to political, economic, and social questions must be at the heart of education for the professions—not as indoctrination, but as moral debate. (Goodlad, 1984, p. 302)

Ethical Dimensions of Professionalism

It is clear from this quotation that professions are not merely occupations with social status; there are ethical and sociopolitical dimensions to achieving and maintaining the status of a profession. An implicit expectation of professionals is that they carry responsibility and trust to maintain certain standards. The standards relate not only to technical competence and expected functions in society but also to professional integrity. Usually the notion of professional integrity refers to a relationship of trust and confidentiality between the professional and the client, which contributes toward the successful performance of the function of the profession. In the education profession, all participants or all students, regardless of their backgrounds or category memberships, are our clients. It thus behoves us as professionals to nurture and protect that relationship for every participant or student. How many of us achieve this?

Similarly, professional ethics affect professionals' relationships with each other. The ultimate end of professional ethics between colleagues is to maintain mutual trust and collaboration within the profession. The achievement of mutual trust is, however, not merely a functional outcome of prescribed modes of behaviour: It is also dependent upon professionals genuinely and explicitly valuing each other's work and contributions, however varied. In the absence of mutual trust and valuing, fragmentation and separation is likely, and outsiders will legitimately see the claims for professionalism as merely a group's protection of vested interests.

Challenges to Professionalism

There have been several challenges and problems with which our profession has had to cope over the last 10 years or so, including the following:

- The general context of public unease with the atmosphere and mission of education, and the decline in funding and the resource base
- The decline of time for physical education in the curricula of many secondary schools; Her Majesty's Inspectors of Schools in the UK have commented that the 5% of curriculum time suggested by Mr Baker, formerly Secretary of State for Education, a suggestion that gave rise to such a furor, is already a fair estimate of the state of affairs in many secondary schools' upper years
- The diversity and fragmentation of programme, ethos and philosophy within the profession, and the increase in responsibility of sporting bodies for educational purposes
- In higher education, the perceived paramount importance of academic aspects of physical education, with claims that this has been at the expense of the pedagogic and professional bases of our subject
- The erosion of conditions of employment and self-regulating control of the profession
- The erosion of teachers' morale in a market economy
- The difficulty of finding a common image with which the outside world can identify

The Commission of Enquiry of the PEA (1987) underlined this last point, the report alluding to the failure of the profession to articulate a philosophy or aim for physical education that is meaningful to parents, children and the general public, or even to reach any consensus within the profession.

If physical educationists have failed to convince the public that there is a common currency in their product and even to decide among themselves what that distinctive feature is, then it is hardly surprising that, even in the most recent publication of curriculum practice (National Curriculum Council [NCC], 1989), only one school purporting to be working towards equal opportunities had done more than decide that mixed physical education was 'the answer'. In other cases, coeducational physical education was adopted without apparent consideration of any of the complex issues, processes and ethics involved. Is this a symptom of a reluctance within physical education to think in abstract terms?

Human Studies and Reflective Professionals

For example, Alison Dewar and Alan Ingham (1987) have outlined the way in which American students in physical education and related disciplines undervalue the human studies in relation to the physical sciences and even question their relevance to their own professional training.

> A lot of people find it off the wall and sort of sit back in their chair, drop their pens and wonder who is this guy. You know, where's he coming from, did he have too much coffee this morning? (p. 10)

This leads an outside observer to ask whether these and our own students are required, as part of their higher education, to confront some of the ethical and social issues that form the context for and influence their future profession. If this is not a crucial and central part of their professional education, this is surely a cause for concern. If nothing else, it would explain why the human studies are so undervalued by undergraduate students—and this at a time when our rapidly changing social world makes it essential that future professionals possess the conceptual and reasoning tools to make rational and ethical decisions.

Physical Education Engendered?

It is also necessary to examine the 'gendering' of physical education as a profession.

> A closer look at institutions where scholarship is created reveals that there are unequal distributions of resources within them, power relationships between dominant and subordinate groups, beliefs and attitudes that define the work of some as more legitimate than others, and socialisation processes by which newcomers are taught the ways of the system. And just as in other institutions, for those who do not conform, a variety of sanctions can be applied, ranging from ridicule to exclusion. (Andersen, 1983, p. 224)

However well defined a professional code is, there will always be occasions when professionals have conflicts and divergent pressures and must resort to their own moral resources. But without an adequate grasp of value positions or without the necessary sense of responsibility, having technical ability and expertise leads to the inconsistent and partial decisions that together become the root cause of accusations of incompetence or unprofessional behaviour. The area of equal opportunity is one for which basic guidelines may be provided, but it is so complex that proper training and education in the moral principles and practical strategies underlying educational practice is a necessity for the would-be professional.

Primarily, the profession must examine its own structures, procedures and practices and work towards valuing the contributions of its various constituent members, even as it addresses the broader issues of widening the franchise of physical education across the school population. The lack of parity of women in the physical education profession is still not recognized as a problem by many people within the profession. Reasons given for their lack of parity centre on the traditional explanations of family responsibility and never on the procedures and practices of the organizations concerned, which in fact inhibit or prevent equal opportunity for women. There has been little attempt to examine the effects of the assumptions of 'possession' of knowledge and expertise in physical education; the sociology of knowledge in this area is relatively undeveloped, except by Ann Hall in the Canadian context. An example of 'gender-blind', 'masculinity-as-culture' curriculum construction and reification is Len Almond's (1989) recently published reader, whose contributors seem not to have recognized any of the central issues surrounding gender and equality. For example, in one chapter (Smith, 1989), the author appears to be unaware that the men whom he names as major influences on the teaching of gymnastics themselves owed much to women physical educationists, whom he fails to mention or of whose existence he is unaware.

It is simply illogical (even immoral?) for a professional group to express the ideology of equality of opportunity for children and students while failing to recognize the effects of its own restrictive practices both on female professionals and on the children at the delivery end of the profession. Similarly, the nature of qualifications and expectations of experience are commonly applied criteria that are ripe for rigorous analysis and review. For example, I have always found it ironic that in Britain teachers may receive incremental allowances for armed service but not for child rearing. Is it really more relevant to learn how to kill than to bring up young children?

Dangers of Professionalism

Terry Johnson (1984) has argued that increasing professionalism and specialization can be viewed by many as a mixed blessing and even as a threat to individual freedom. It is arguable that the professional actually undermines the power of individuals to take responsibility for their own development and well-being. Johnson argues that, partly because of the diversity of professions (and physical education and sport are certainly diverse) and partly because of the struggle of new occupational groups to achieve status and recognition, professionalism has tended to become an occupational ideal in a society whose technological advances continually erode the mystique that traditionally supported the esoteric and exclusive nature of professional knowledge. In such a situation, Johnson argues, insight into the relationship of professions' status and their access to knowledge must take account of the power relations through which access and control are achieved and maintained. One of the dangers of professions achieving degrees of maintenance and control is that professions find themselves, even when beleaguered by social pressures, inflexible or unable to change. They may therefore perpetuate forms of power relations that are out of date and out of step with the rest of society (like colonies of dinosaurs). The more uncertain the status of the profession, the less likely it is that it will be willing and able to manage change.

A Widening Knowledge Gap

Professions whose status is uncertain attempt to widen the knowledge gap between themselves and their clients in order to reestablish and reinforce their professionalism. This widening of the knowledge gap can take several forms, which may be identifiable in our own profession: increasing specialization and depth of enquiry; entering into co-operation or collusion with more established disciplines, often resulting in a distancing from the original intention; adopting and mastering the new technologies that have the potential to make the profession's subject matter more accessible to others, but in order to control that means of access; lengthening the period of professional education and increasing the strictures surrounding the profession; and adopting more exclusive and inflexible entry requirements, often on the pretext of 'protecting standards'. Where mystification occurs, it may be a cause for questioning its necessity, rather than as a means of maintaining self-image and status in a beleaguered world.

> Professional education, as it exists at a particular moment in time, is then the sediment of the former struggles and strategies of occupations for whom the images of success survive from an heroic past, and it is the continuing contemporary vigour of professionalism as a strategy which generates the heat fusing such sediment into the rocks on which educational innovation and reform so often founders. (Johnson, 1984, p. 25)

Dewar and Ingham (1987) likewise conclude that

> our data reinforce the idea that professionalism can negate or at least undermine the culture of critical discourse as defined in humanistic intellectualist terms. . . . we would add that professionalism may drive a wedge between the two groups . . . (the humanistic intellectuals and the technical intelligentsia) at least as far as students' perceptions of really useful knowledge are concerned. (p. 11)

> We in physical education have spent decades questing after authority. The quest is professionalist and the quest stifles critical evaluation, creative problem formation and crap detecting. (p. 13)

Gatekeeping in Physical Education

It might be an illuminating exercise to compare the previous comments with the development of physical education in higher education and even the ways in which school examinations in physical education have been evolved. It might be a painful process, but it could also be a profitable one. In particular, a useful diagnostic method might be to analyse on what conditions and by what criteria newcomers to the profession achieve success. Is the route to success narrow and rigidly defined? How varied are the career paths of the people in the profession who are seen as the models for others? How often is it the case that newcomers achieve success (or even parity) only when they adopt and practise the prevailing procedures and practices? How does the profession respond to challenge and criticism? Who are the gatekeepers of the profession, how do they operate, and from what sources do they attain their power and influence?

'Gatekeeping' is an extremely useful term: It refers to particular people setting standards, making decisions and monitoring what counts as knowledge, and identifying what is seen as innovatory. Liz Stanley (1984) has identified the contribution of gatekeepers in the processes of academic professional control. She argues that the notion of gatekeeping is more useful than that of social control because gatekeepers often act, with the best of motives, to protect what is seen to be right and correct rather than as deliberate seekers of power. She analyses the processes of gatekeeping in discriminating against feminist researchers and academics and advocates a confrontation with conventional social science: 'Confrontation is never pleasant; but then neither is covert, disguised and politically-motivated discrimination against women and against feminism nor incorporation and accommodation among erstwhile revolutionaries' (p. 207).

Confronting Discrimination

In Britain it has often been remarked that antisexist education has been dragged into action 'on the coat-tails of antiracist education'. There are so many common factors. Learning new perspectives is rarely comfortable. I quote now from *Cry Freedom*, a novel based on the life and death of Steven Biko, the Bantu leader who died in a South African prison; a white journalist's attempts to understand a new point of view are being described.

> [Woods] glanced from Biko to the others. 'You put all the words together well—but there's something about it that scares me.'
>
> 'Of course there is,' Mapetla responded. 'In your world everything "white" is "normal"—the way the world is supposed to be—and everything black is "wrong" or some kind of mistake.'
>
> The others chorused agreement.
>
> 'And your real genius,' Biko added, 'is that for decades you've managed to convince most of *us* of that too.'
>
> Woods grinned, but he felt that the comment wasn't the whole truth. 'You're being unfair to a lot of people who—'
>
> But Biko didn't let him finish. 'In fact our case is very simple,' he said quietly. 'We believe in an *intelligent* God. We believe He knew what He was doing

when He made the black man . . . Just as He did when He made the white man . . .'

He held Woods' gaze and the profundity and godlike neutrality underlying those words affected Woods more than anything he had seen that whole eventful day. (Briley, 1987, p. 67)

We need to remember that feeling inadequate in a new situation or with a new challenge is not a matter of shame, merely a need to learn new insights and skills and to understand ourselves better. Questioning established practices involves examining hitherto inviolate and taken-for-granted customs and the possibility of a dominant group's losing status or exclusive privilege. It also constitutes a risk that performance previously regarded as successful and 'good practice' may lose its currency because of the application of new criteria. When prevailing assumptions are challenged, there is often genuine surprise and resentment.

Institutionalised sexism is harder to identify since it is a result of rules, regulations, and traditions that may not result directly from the decisions of one or more sexists. But the rules, regulations and traditions end up supporting a sexist ideology. (Frieze, Parsons, Johnson, Ruble, & Zellman, 1978, p. 13)

Rules and norms that ignore the different life experience and contributions of women or black, disabled or gay people may be continued in blind (or wilfully blind) adherence to 'normal' practice. Social norms remain 'envalued'.

One of the conventional defences of professional bodies, when challenged to demonstrate their progress in the area of equality of opportunity, is to explain lack of parity as part of a wider social situation over which they have no control. But this is to deny that a profession has any control over its own affairs or any power to change society—surely elements that theoretically characterize professions! In any case, it is worth remembering that we have to assess not whether we can be sure of success—a rare expectation in education—but whether it is *worth trying*.

Conclusion

Adoption of suitable strategies to achieve change always causes disagreement. But it is for each group of physical education professionals to work out their own appropriate strategies, with the ultimate aim of giving real opportunities to all people—regardless of their gender, age, sexuality, ethnicity or social background—to experience the kind of physical awareness and self-knowledge that can be achieved by sensitive and intelligent participation in physical activity. I should like to illustrate this with two quotations, the first from a beautifully written account of an all-female expedition to Annapurna, where the group attempted to demonstrate belief in feminist principles even after two of their number were lost.

Fortunately we had not simply buried our hurt feelings and gone marching stoically up the mountain. It had been worth it to take the time to face up to each other and expose our vulnerability, hurt, and anger, and then our fears. We realized again how much we cared about each other, and our shared laughter had been the final healing touch. (Blum, 1980, p. 119)

The second quotation is by Gwen Moffat (1961), capturing eloquently her moment of revelation about her climbing and her body, a moment caused by her pregnancy and increased awareness of what she was doing.

I told them I was having a baby in July. Consternation! Most of the club were on the cliff (including several doctors) and messages were relayed from climb to climb, and up and down the ropes, to the effect that Moffat was having a baby and what was the quickest way to get her off the cliff? One would have thought I was about to be confined on the Great Terrace. . . .

I refused to be stampeded. I had come to the meet to join the club if possible and I was going to lead my climb to qualify. Besides, since we were on the Great Terrace, I pointed out that the easiest way off was to climb. So I led Red Wall and Longland's Continuation—barefooted of course—while a frieze of Pinnaclers sat on the top and watched critically. I felt like a cripple who rediscovers his body while swimming. Here on the airy slabs of those two delightful climbs, where the holds are one-toe holds in places and the run-outs are long, I could forget for a while my pear-shape and feel the old elegance. And, not illogically, there flashed through my mind the hope that the baby would be a girl. (pp. 120-121)

These moments are what physical education ultimately is about—experiences as diverse as life itself—and we need to learn to appreciate and value them all. As my colleague Sheila Scraton (1986) has written,

For 'physical' power relations and, ultimately, the politics of patriarchy to be challenged, girls and young women should be encouraged to enjoy physical movement on *their* terms and develop confidence, assertiveness and control over their own bodies. (p. 91)

Surely this is the ultimate aim of physical education, for all children. If physical education is structured and operated in such a way that all children are not afforded this opportunity, it is time for us to begin looking to those structures and processes—and to our own attitudes.

References

Alberta Education. (1988). *Physical education grades 7-12 curriculum*. Edmonton, Alberta, Cananda: Alberta Education.

Almond, L. (Ed.) (1989). *The place of physical education in schools*. London: Kogan Page.

Andersen, M.L. (1983). *Thinking about women*. New York: Macmillan.

Blum, A. (1980). *Annapurna: A woman's place*. Manchester: Granada Press.

Briley, J. (1987). *Cry Freedom*. London: Penguin Books.

Butcher, J. (1983). Issues concerning girls' sports participation during childhood and adolescence. *Canadian Women's Studies, 4*, 43-46.

Dewar, A., & Ingham, A. (1987). Really useful knowledge: Professionalist interests, critical discourse, student responses. In *Congress on movement and sport in women's life*. Symposium conducted at the University of Jyvaskyla, Finland.

Dunbar, R., & O'Sullivan, M. (1986). Effects of intervention on differential treatment of boys and girls in elementary physical education lessons. *Journal of Teaching in Physical Education, 5*, 166-175.

Evans, J. (1989). *Equality and opportunity in the physical education curriculum*. Unpublished paper.

Evans, J., & Clarke, G. (1988). Changing the face of teachers, teaching and control. In J. Evans (Ed.), *Teachers, Teaching and Control in Physical Education*. Brighton: Falmer Press.

Evans, J., & Davies, B. (1988). Introduction: Teachers, teaching and control. In J. Evans (Ed.), *Teachers, teaching and control in physical education*. Brighton: Falmer Press.

Evans, J., Lopez, S., Duncan, M., & Evans, M. (1987). Some thoughts on the political and pedagogical implications of mixed sex grouping in the physical education curriculum. *British Educational Research Journal, 13*, 59-71.

Fletcher, S. (1984). *Women first*. Cambridge: Athlone Press.

Frieze, I.H., Parsons, J.E., Johnson, P.B., Ruble, D.N., & Zellman, G.L. (1978). *Women and sex roles: A social psychological perspective*. New York: W.W. Norton.

Gibbon, A. (1988). Editorial. *British Journal of Physical Education, 19*, 147.

Girls measure up. (1989, April 9). *Sunday Times*, p. 11.

Goodlad, S. (Ed.) (1984). *Education for the professions. Quis custodiet?* Guildford, Surrey: Society for Research into Higher Education/National Foundation for Educational Research; Nelson.

Green, S.J.D. (1988). Is equality of opportunity a false ideal for society? *British Journal of Sociology, 39*, 1-27.

Hall, M.A. (1987). Masculinity as culture: The discourse of gender and sport. In *Congress on Movement and sport in women's life*. Symposium conducted at the University of Jyvaskyla, Finland.

Johnson, T. (1984). Professionalism: Occupation or ideology? In S. Goodlad (Ed.), *Education for the professions. Quis custodiet?* Guildford, Surrey: Society for Research into Higher Education/National Foundation for Educational Research; Nelson.

Moffat, G. (1961). *Space below my feet*. London: Hodder and Stoughton.

National Curriculum Council. (1989). *Physical education: Recent curriculum developments*. York: School Curriculum Development Committee.

Peters, R.S. (1966). *Ethics and education*. London: Allen & Unwin.

Physical Education Association. (1987). Physical education in schools. London: Ling.

Scraton, S. (1986). Images of femininity and the teaching of girls' physical education. In J. Evans (Ed.), *Physical education, sport and schooling: Studies in the sociology of physical education*. Brighton: Falmer Press.

Scraton, S. (1990). 'One step forward, two steps back': The implications for girls of mixed physical education. In S. Scraton (Ed.), *Gender and physical education*. Victoria, Australia: Deakin University Press.

Smith, B. (1989). Curriculum developments in gymnastics. In L. Almond (Ed.), *The place of physical education in schools*. London: Kogan Page.

Solesbury, W. (1976, Winter). The environmental agenda. *Public Administration*.

Sparkes, A. (1987). *Innovation in physical education*. Paper presented to meeting of Standing Conference of Physical Education in Teacher Education, Woolley Hall, Wakefield.

Stanley, L. (1984). How the social science research process discriminates against women. In S. Acker & D. Piper (Eds.), *Is higher education fair to women?* Guildford, Surrey: Society for Research in Higher Education/National Foundation for Educational Research; Nelson.

Talbot, M. (1988). 'Beating them at our own game? Women's sports involvement.' In E. Wimbush & M. Talbot (Eds.), *Relative freedoms: Women and leisure*. Milton Keynes: Open University Press.

Turvey, J., & Laws, C. (1988). 'Are girls losing out?' The effects of mixed-sex grouping on girls' performance in physical education. *British Journal of Physical Education*, **19**, 253-255.

Walker, J.C. (1988). The way men act: Dominant and subordinate male cultures in an inner-city school. *British Journal of Sociology of Education, 9*, 3-18.

Chapter 7

Physical Education for Children With Severe Learning Difficulties

Michael Alcott

*There's nobody on our staff who is qualified in PE. We do a little
bit of apparatus, a bit of football . . . that's about it.*

So said a teacher in a school for pupils with severe learning difficulties (SLD).
The year: 1989. Such evidence as is available suggests that far too many schools
for pupils with SLD are delivering an inadequate physical education curriculum.
By contrast, a minority are doing excellent work, and their pupils reap the benefits.

Introduction

In this chapter I shall look at physical education in schools for pupils with severe
learning difficulties. Having first identified the range of pupils and legislation
relating to them, I shall outline current provision and put forward suggestions
about possible future developments.

The Pupils

Definition

Pupils with severe learning difficulties are still widely referred to as being mentally
handicapped. In the educational world the concept 'mental handicap' has been
replaced by the concept 'severe learning difficulties'. Warnock (1978) took the
innovative step of turning attention away from the handicap and focusing on the
children's educability when she determined that 'children with severe learning
difficulties is our preferred description of those children who are commonly
referred to as being mentally handicapped' (p. 220). That was an important shift

of emphasis. The level of labeling has moved from the turn of the century's 'imbecile' and 'idiot', through the phase of 'subnormality', to current dropping of labels and accepting pupils as full members of the human family with one particularity: learning difficulties of a severe degree.

Warnock (1978), in the wake of the 1970 Education Act, underlined the point that this particular group of neglected, socially invisible people could be educated and, in consequence, be visible, participant members of society. But to what levels? Almost a decade after Warnock, Cambridgeshire County Council (1987) put one Local Education Authority's (LEA's) interpretation on the concept, stating that children with 'severe learning difficulties' were

> those children whose learning difficulties are so severe and complex that they are unlikely ever to be able to live completely independent adult lives.
>
> The term covers a considerable range of ability; at one end the most profoundly handicapped require almost constant physical care and supervision, while at the other, there are individuals who can manage the more straightforward tasks of day to day living if they are given guidance on how to organise themselves. (p. 1)

Let us make things clear. We are talking about people who may have, amongst other medical conditions, Down's Syndrome, cerebral palsy, Prader-Willi Syndrome, phenylketonuria, autism and mental retardation* of unspecified aetiology. They may have other complicating factors such as sensory handicaps and metabolic disorders. As a result, they may be profoundly or multiply handicapped.

Qualities

The range of qualities displayed by this varied group of people is considerable. As Her Majesty's Stationery Office (1975) suggested, their behaviour can range from passive to hyperactive, from consistent to inconsistent; they may have minimal motor ability or be quite reasonably coordinated and active; their response to language may be nil, or they may have good comprehension; their vocalization may be limited to random noises or may consist of perfectly satisfactory speech; they may have specific disabilities in perception along with sensory and motor impairments.

It is of particular importance to teachers of physical education that, compared with 'normal' pupils, pupils with SLD record poorer scores on body size, flexibility, strength, endurance, motor coordination and motor skills generally (Gordon, Sugden, & Fryer, 1982). Their lack of high-quality physical education in school could in part cause some of these results. We are in the realm of the nature versus nurture question. Experience suggests that many pupils with SLD can make great improvements in some of these areas when they are put on varied, developmental physical education programmes.

---

*See the appendix for brief descriptions of these conditions.

Incidence

Statham et al. (1989) pointed out that in England in 1985 there were 19,700 boys and 14,000 girls following developmental curricula in special schools.

Legislation

The Education (Handicapped Children) Act of 1970

This Act paved the way for the integration of people with mental handicaps into society. Prior to 1970 they were under the care of the health authorities. Generally speaking, they were either living in long-stay hospitals or spending their days in junior training centres. The 1970 Act boldly stated that it was 'an Act to make provision, as respects England and Wales, for discontinuing the classification of handicapped children as unsuitable for education at school' [The Education (Handicapped Children) Act, 1970, p. 5]. Prior to this Act children with mental handicap were removed from society and made socially invisible. The 1970 Act put an end to 'classifying children suffering from a disability of mind as children unsuitable for education at school'.

In 1971, following the Act, local education authorities took over from health authorities the responsibility for children then categorized as mentally handicapped. As a result, 'some 24,000 children in junior training centres and special care units, 8,000 in about 100 hospitals, and an uncertain number at home or in private institutions ceased to be treated as being mentally deficient and became entitled to special education' (Warnock, 1978).

That was a turning point for improving the quality of life of so many people labeled mentally handicapped. Junior training centres became schools; purpose-built schools appeared. The curriculum for pupils with mental handicaps became a matter for professional interest. But more was to come. The eighties saw the next step forward with the 1981 Education Act.

The Education Act of 1981

This Act implemented the recommendations of the Warnock Committee (1978). The focus was on considering the special educational needs of pupils and the integration of pupils with SLD into mainstream schools.

Integration

Integration has been a dominant concern over the past decade for people involved in the education of children with SLD. As Warnock (1978) had made clear, integration is a process with various stages: locational, social, functional. Much ink has been used and much rhetoric employed in promoting the cause of integration. It has to be said that the functional integration of pupils with SLD into mainstream schools has had limited success. At the primary level it can work well; at the secondary level it is a process that is fraught with difficulties.

Some people would say that progress would have been swifter over the past 6 years if government had shown 100% commitment to the integration of people with special educational needs into society. The Metropolitan Authorities (Education, Science and Arts Committee, 1986–87) were unequivocal in their assessment of the government attitude to integration. Commenting on the Act, they said, 'The unwillingness of central government to accept the resource implications of the legislation has also inhibited substantial progress in implementing the Act' (p. 6).

Current Practice

Where Pupils With SLD Are Schooled

Since the 1981 Act the response of local authorities to the call for integration of children with special needs into mainstream schools has been quite varied. A handful of LEAs have worked with energy and enthusiasm to ensure effective integration; the majority have made rather half-hearted attempts; a number have actually increased segregated provision.

However, the very fact of LEA wavering has allowed enthusiastic teachers to establish their own mini-integration schemes. Many special schools for pupils with severe learning difficulties have made contact with neighbourhood mainstream schools. In some instances this has led to locational and social integration. It has also led to the development of a two-way educational process, with mainstream pupils venturing into special schools. An important meeting point has often been physical education, with shared games, swimming and dance. A primary school teacher observed, reflecting on her experience of having a boy with Down's Syndrome in her class for part of the week, 'In many ways it is easier to cope with him in P.E. rather than in the classroom. In P.E. he can watch others, copy their movements. In the classroom, the need for fine motor skills, the use of pencils, reading, writing, number work are all more difficult for him to deal with.'

Encouraging as many integration schemes are, the truth is that overall there appears to have been little change since the late seventies. Warnock (1978) reported that 'the majority of these children [SLD] are at present educated in day special schools or hospital schools, although a few units for them have been set up in ordinary primary and secondary schools' (p. 221). A decade later, after legislation, so many books, campaigns and hours of lectures, the majority of pupils with special needs are still educated in special schools. Statham (1989), drawing on Department of Education and Science (DES) statistics, calculated that in 1986 74% of all statemented children were in special schools, 12% in special classes in 'ordinary' schools, and a mere 7% in ordinary classes in ordinary schools. It is probable that of that 7%, very few are pupils with SLD.

When considering the current position with reference to physical education and pupils with severe learning difficulties, it is the provision in special schools that is the main focus of attention.

Special Schools and Their Facilities

Special schools share certain characteristics and differ from mainstream schools in important ways (Statham, 1989). They are nearly always small, with 88% having fewer than 125 pupils; many cover the age range of 3 to 19 years; teacher-pupil ratios are high, 1:6.8 in 1985. Of the total number of special schools in the UK, 17.7% are for pupils with severe learning difficulties.

It is in these small, all-age, well-staffed schools that the majority of pupils with SLD are educated. What is the curriculum like and how does physical education fit into it?

Curriculum Concerns in the Special School

The DES/Welsh Office (1984) has suggested that pupils who have severe learning difficulties need a developmental curriculum, 'a curriculum covering selected and sharply focussed educational, social and other experiences with precisely defined objectives and designed to encourage a measure of personal autonomy' (p. 2). That statement leaves ample scope for physical education in the curriculum. However, this *Note* continues with less than favourable implications.

> The developmental approach puts the main emphasis upon enabling pupils to take a part in and derive satisfaction from the society in which they live to the greatest extent possible. The basic elements of this approach should be the acquisition of communication, self help, mobility and social skills, very basic literacy and numeracy, and an understanding of the world about them including simple science in its application to everyday life.

That is a prescription for a rather arid curriculum. It is to be noted that the richness, variety and life-enhancing potential of physical education is reduced to a single concept, 'mobility'.

Warnock (1978) also drew attention to the curricular needs of pupils with profound or multiple handicaps, many of whom are educated in SLD schools. Their needs can best be met by multidisciplinary provision.

> They require a form of special education which necessitates intimate collaboration between doctors, nurses, teachers, therapists of all kinds and psychologists, so that programmes can be devised which build on the slightest responses elicited from individuals. (p. 221)

It should now be evident that physical education, as traditionally understood by specialists and professional bodies, appears to have little acknowledged place in the curriculum for pupils with SLD. The findings of Gordon et al. (1982), based on an extensive survey just before the implementation of the 1981 Education Act, only served to show the reality of this official neglect. There may have been some changes since then, but they have had little impact on physical education in schools for pupils with SLD. Their survey indicated a very sorry picture: schools with inadequate gymnasia, lacking playing fields, poorly resourced and, most important, lacking specialist physical education teachers or even regular staff with a minimum of physical education training.

Their findings relevant to this issue are worth reporting in detail. Using pre-Warnock terminology, they are summarized as follows (my subheadings and italics throughout):

On the curriculum
The Brennan (1979) study examined many curricular areas of which physical education was one. It reported that *only 15% of the special schools surveyed (N=75) were classed as having a successful curriculum for physical education.*

On teachers of PE
In over 70% of E.S.N. [educationally sub-normal] (M—moderate) and E.S.N. (S—severe) schools *at least 40% of the teachers had no training in physical education at university, college or on any supplementary courses.* . . . 92% of physical education in E.S.N. (S) schools was taught by the classroom teacher and 22% by a physical education specialist, with 29% indicating both.

On resources
Less than 10% of E.S.N. (S) schools have purpose built gymnasiums. . . . On site fields are provided in only 57% of (S) schools. (Gordon et al., 1982, pp. 138-140)

If we bring together the various findings so far presented, we have a group of pupils who are not being integrated into mainstream schools in any great numbers. They do not have access to specialist physical education staff and the range of primary or comprehensive school facilities. In the special schools where they are being educated, the curricula do not usually give prominence to physical education, specialist physical education staff are rare and facilities are often inadequate. Clearly, many pupils with severe learning difficulties are deprived of well-structured, professionally delivered physical education curricula.

And yet there may be hope. In spite of the less than enthusiastic support for physical education in official documents and the unimpressive staffing and facilities in the schools, Gordon et al. (1982) noted that attitudes of teachers working in those very schools were generally positive. They said that 'it is interesting to note that all schools with a PE specialist thought them beneficial.' They concluded that 'more than 80% of all E.S.N. teachers see physical, social, cognitive and emotional development positively affected by physical education' (pp. 138-140).

Moving forward to 1987, the Physical Education Association of Great Britain and Northern Ireland stated that 'within GB in particular, there still appears to be a lack of appreciation of the important role of physical education in the all-round development of all children but in particular of children with special educational needs'' (PEA, 1987, p. 100). All of this is puzzling in a decade that has seen the Health Education Authority and influential sections of the physical education profession promoting and lauding the benefits of an active lifestyle and health-related fitness.

More than puzzling, it is unacceptable. Pupils with severe learning difficulties, who have limited access to many areas of human experience, can gain immense benefits from a skilfully taught physical education curriculum, benefits that can last them a lifetime.

Content of the Physical Education Curriculum

Against this discouraging background, we can take a closer look at what is being taught in the schools. Obviously there is considerable variation in both the quantity and quality of what is being offered to pupils with SLD. The data and quotes in this section are drawn from the survey by Gordon et al. (1982).

Most schools do something, however modest. Swimming is by far the most popular activity (in over 88% of schools). This includes therapy for pupils with profound and multiple handicaps, regular swimming lessons and recreation. Some schools have their own heated indoor pools. It is likely that in many instances the therapeutic value of water activity, encouraged by physiotherapists, has been the starting point for a swimming programme. Nowadays, an ever-increasing number of pupils visit public pools for swimming sessions.

Adapted games come next in popularity, with over 64% of schools offering them. There is no doubt a range of small games, some of the major games such as soccer and cricket, other team games such as volleyball and hockey, along with badminton and tennis. These are adapted in a variety of ways to meet the needs and abilities of the pupils.

There is also likely a focus on developing and improving basic gross and fine motor skills. This was ranked as the primary objective by over 56% of schools. The objective is often achieved by providing pupils with a circuit of apparatus for balancing, climbing, jumping and so on. Some schools offer pupils the opportunity to develop these basic skills on play apparatus, on challenge courses and in adventure playgrounds. Pony riding, a popular activity in many schools, is also legitimized in the curriculum, in part for its contribution to the improvement of motor skills (the development of sitting, balance, strengthening postural muscles etc.).

After swimming, adapted games and motor skill development, the physical education curriculum may take a sharp nosedive in many schools. Gymnastics, dance and games occupy 10% to 14% of the physical education curriculum in all schools, and athletics a mere 2% to 3%. Over 50% of (S) schools 'ranked recreation last or did not rank it at all' (p. 140). This is surprising for schools where the curriculum is designed to meet the needs of pupils. One thing that the majority of pupils with SLD have, and will have throughout their lives, is an excess of leisure time.

Whilst the overall picture of provision is not impressive, there is room for restrained optimism. We must bear in mind that few senior members of the physical education profession had any in-depth preparation for teaching pupils with SLD. And yet there is a minority of schools offering pupils excellent physical education programmes. These are the schools where there is usually an enthusiastic physical education specialist, supported by an enlightened headteacher and aided by keen staff, who is given every encouragement to develop physical education to the full.

With a curriculum freed from the restraints of examination syllabuses, the physical education curricula in this minority of schools are restricted only by the expertise and resources that are available. I can now sketch in some of the activities found in these schools.

Activities Offered in Special Schools

There is a commitment to health-related fitness. The development of gross motor skills is fundamental, covering the range from the needs of pupils who are totally dependent on others for movement to the needs of those who can learn the sophisticated perceptual-motor skills required for a host of sporting activities. There is co-operation between the school and visiting paediatric physiotherapists. Fine motor skills are also developed, often with input from an occupational therapist.

Many of these schools include some form of gymnastics, music and movement, and various types of dance. There is an increasing interest in yoga and relaxation techniques. Trampolines are often used, for two distinct activities. First, supported by the award scheme of the British Trampoline Federation, there is straightforward trampolining. Second, there is rebound therapy. In this, pupils with SLD and, in particular, those with profound/multiple handicaps can enjoy the stimulation of the trampoline's rebound qualities.

The name of Veronica Sherborne is well known to many teachers working with pupils who have severe learning difficulties. This former physical education and dance lecturer developed an approach to movement interaction for pupils and staff that is known the world over as Sherborne Movement. It is widely practised in special schools.

Swimming, as we have seen, features on the curriculum of many schools. Some schools follow the Halliwick Method, developed to meet the needs of pupils with physical handicaps and named after the Halliwick School, London, where it was created in 1949. It is characterized by the absence of all artificial flotation aids and by one-to-one teaching.

The major team games, central to the mainstream physical education curriculum, are rarely dominant. Small numbers of pupils in a class, cognitive difficulties, low levels of perceptual-motor skills and a widespread noncompetitive quality in pupils combine to make games such as soccer, cricket and basketball nonstarters in many schools. Of course, some schools do adapt a range of games very successfully, but they are a small minority.

By contrast, co-operative games are increasingly popular. A parachute canopy is often found in the gym cupboard. It is a magnificent piece of equipment that promotes activity and group co-operation. It is also guaranteed to provide hours of enjoyment.

Athletics includes jogging, some track running, jumps and adapted throwing activities.

A variety of outdoor pursuits feature on the physical education curricula of many schools. Depending on staff enthusiasm and skills, any or all of the following are to be found: canoeing, sailing, cycling, skiing, hiking, camping, backpacking and orienteering. Some schools use outdoor pursuits for personal and social development.

As has already been pointed out, pupils with SLD have many leisure hours at their disposal. Recreation skills, as well as many of the other skills learned in physical education lessons, equip pupils for active integration into their local communities. In schools where staff take notice of this, pupils are given opportunities to acquire and practice recreation skills. These are so important for them, especially when they leave school. There are schools where pupils learn bowls, snooker, archery, golf and skating.

On a more basic and esoteric level, there is Snoezelen. This form of recreation and sensory stimulation originated in Holland. In an enclosed space—a room or a suite of rooms—a multisensory experience is provided. It is particularly designed for people with profound and multiple handicaps. The concept of Snoezelen is gradually becoming known in the UK. A few innovative schools have created snoezelen rooms; a research project in Chesterfield should soon provide data on the benefits of this form of recreational activity.

Integration With Mainstream Schools

In schools where all levels and types of integration have been considered, there is a variety of links with mainstream schools. The physical education curriculum provides many opportunities for social and functional integration. Special school pupils may join in mainstream physical education lessons; they may combine on special projects: camping, dance workshops, residential trips and so on; mainstream pupils may spend time in the special school. These contacts are educational for both parties. Often the mainstream pupils (and staff) discover that their understanding of 'mental handicap' is woefully inaccurate. A group of primary pupils, on a residential week with pupils with severe learning difficulties, came to the experience with a range of curious ideas. They expected to find children in wheelchairs, unable to talk, needing help all the time. By the end of the week, they had discovered that this was not so. 'I was a bit worried', admitted one boy. 'I didn't really know what to expect. I thought they'd be a bit peculiar. I soon got used to them. I was surprised to see how Tony ran up and down the hills. He was much fitter than me.' That admiration, learned on the Cumbrian fells, may colour the boy's attitude to people with disabilities for the rest of his life.

The Contribution of Other Agencies

Whilst the focus of this chapter is on schools, it would be churlish not to mention the excellent work being done by governing bodies, private companies and voluntary agencies. Their activities and intiatives do reach back into the schools and have an effect on curriculum development. The governing bodies of sports are taking steps to meet the needs of people with severe learning difficulties. Often pressured by enthusiasts, they are developing award schemes that are appropriate for this minority population. Private companies, particularly in the outdoor pursuits business, are either offering integrated opportunities to this new range of clients or putting on special courses for them. Associations that cater specifically for people with mental handicap, such as the United Kingdom Sports Association for People with Mental Handicap, Mencap and Special Olympics, are constantly increasing the range of activities on offer and gently promoting integration through sport.

Looking Ahead

Such, then, is the picture of physical education provision for pupils with severe learning difficulties. Some pupils, the minority, enjoy a varied, skilfully delivered curriculum. For the majority, already denied access to many human experiences because of their learning difficulties, physical education provision is totally inadequate. I now look at some of the possible ways of improving physical education for these pupils.

Some Suggestions

Any discussion of future developments must be placed within the context of the Education Reform Act of 1988. We have seen that the integration of pupils with SLD into mainstream schools has been patchy and limited. Today many teachers in special schools consider that the future for integration is bleak. Whilst Warnock (1978) put a timescale of 20 years on full-scale integration, nobody in the early eighties considered that future legislation might inadvertently hinder or reverse the process. We may be entering a decade in which integration will decline and segregated provision will expand.

Against this background of uncertainty, it is important to bear in mind the position of physical education in the total education of pupils with SLD. It is widely supported that all people with special needs should be integrated as fully as possible into society through participation in the activities of their local communities. Physical education has a unique part to play in promoting the fullest possible participation. Physical educators can provide opportunities for pupils to improve their fitness and the performance level of their motor skills, they can provide opportunities for learning many sports and recreation skills, and they can create opportunities for integrated activities at all levels. Thus, physical education can make a major contribution to the present and future lifestyles of these pupils.

In the light of the evidence about present provision, we can make some specific suggestions about ways in which to achieve long-term improvements in physical education for SLD pupils.

Initial Teacher Training

If the physical education delivered to pupils with SLD is to be of a high standard, the schools require staff who have expertise in adapted physical education. It is in the universities and other institutions of higher education that the seeds of this expertise must be sown.

In recent years initial teacher training courses have taken steps to meet this need by introducing relevant course content. The quality varies and is dependent on a number of factors, not the least being the level of expertise of college staff. In addition to gaining basic knowledge of child development and perceptual and motor development, trainee teachers need to learn about the range of disabling conditions, their aetiology and their impact on the educational prospects of pupils; they need to learn and gain familiarity with assessment procedures, curriculum planning and a range of specialized teaching methods; above all, they need classroom contact with a variety of pupils with special needs to dispel myths, allay their fears and instil confidence in dealing with them.

Developing and Sharing Expertise

At present, expertise in physical education for pupils with special needs—and, in particular, pupils with severe learning difficulties—is limited and often inaccessible. Much of the development of expertise has come from the ground up. Enthusiastic teachers in schools have explored the literature, sought out the company of other enthusiasts and made their own imaginative adaptations of standard procedures. All too often these teachers keep their expertise to themselves. In the institutions of higher education, there is a small band of lecturers who have appropriate knowledge and experience that they make available to others through lectures, courses and writings.

There is, therefore, a need to increase depth and breadth of expertise and make it more accessible to specialist teachers of physical education and nonspecialists who teach physical education in primary, secondary or special schools. After strong foundations have been laid during initial training, teachers must look to in-service training for courses that will extend their knowledge and expertise. Whilst bodies such as the PEA, some private agencies and a small number of LEAs do organize courses on special needs from time to time, much more has to be done if the oft-expressed need for guidance is to be fully met.

We need to increase contact with colleagues overseas so that we do not waste time and resources reinventing the wheel. We need to see far more research and writing about adapted physical education in general. We need more staff in institutions of higher education with greater expertise that they can pass on to students. And we need to create an atmosphere in which student teachers consider expertise in adapted physical education to be worthwhile in professional and career terms.

A national body to store, update and deliver the expertise would be a great advance. Although it is too early for us to be anything other than cautious, the recently formed International Centre for Information and Study of Special Needs

Education at the Institute of Education, London, may fulfil this function. If this centre does live up to its name and include physical education, it could become a powerful force for the development and sharing of expertise.

In the Schools

The conversion of this expertise into curriculum content for the pupils is the raison d'être for this entire educational edifice. There is a degree of complexity that makes straightforward propositions tricky. We have to consider both the integrated and the segregated settings, both the primary and the secondary phases. In primary schools it is usual for the class teacher to teach physical education. That teacher is not often a physical education specialist, though he or she may well have given special emphasis to physical education during initial training. In the secondary schools it is usual for physical education to be taught by specialists. In the special schools, as we have seen, it is rare for specialist physical education teachers to be found, even though pupils may stay there through the secondary years. Gordon et al. (1982) discovered a widespread need for such specialists. With 70% of teachers in special schools expressing a positive attitude to having a physical education specialist on the staff, they commented, 'On every staff there ought to be a specialist in physical education, who not necessarily teaches all the physical education, but who could organise the curriculum throughout the school and act in an advisory capacity to the rest of the staff.'

If it is so obvious that special schools need specialist physical education teachers, then two linked developments have to happen. First, LEAs must accept the proposition and be prepared to staff schools accordingly. Second, specialist physical education teachers must be encouraged to consider a career in which they specialize in adapted physical education.

Curriculum Development

A better prepared body of teachers is the key to any improvements in the quality of physical education delivered to pupils with severe learning difficulties, be they in mainstream or special schools. These teachers will develop curricular aims and content that are appropriate to the needs and abilities of the pupils and that can be related to the demands of the National Curriculum, an important dimension.

Resources

As I have indicated, the resourcing of many special schools is lamentable. As long as the special schools exist—and, however modified, they are likely to be part of the educational scene for many years to come—then efforts should be made to improve their facilities. Of course, many hands are held out for the financial support of LEAs, but a strong case can be made for making provision for pupils with SLD. After all, they do not ask for expensive facilities such as language laboratories, science laboratories, engineering workshops and well-stocked libraries.

Outside Agencies

A number of agencies are doing excellent work for and with people who have severe learning difficulties. The Special Olympics movement, for example, is becoming increasingly well known for its promotion of sporting activities at the local and international levels. The Outward Bound Trust, YMCA, Ocean Youth Club, UK Sports Association for People With Mental Handicap, Riding for the Disabled and many more organizations all have much to offer. An ever-increasing number of governing bodies are developing award schemes for pupils with special needs. Schools can gain much for their pupils by developing links with as wide a range of sporting bodies as possible.

Campaigning

Campaigning—sounding the trumpet for the value of physical education for pupils with SLD and for the satisfaction of teaching them—is an important activity. The message needs to be stated and frequently repeated: Physical education must be central to the educational experience of children who have severe learning difficulties. This message needs to be put to staff in schools; to lecturers in institutions of higher education; to administrators, LEA officers and politicians. Mainstream teachers and students must be given every opportunity to visit special schools, to gain experience with pupils who have SLD, and to see for themselves that teaching this particular group of pupils makes demands and challenges but also offers rewards and job satisfaction. Attitudes have to be modified, enthusiasm generated. Progress depends on the expectations, encouragement and energies of those who care for and educate these children.

Final Word

Progress is possible. Changes can be made. If politicians, parents and educators have the will to improve physical education for children who have severe learning difficulties, then improvements will come. Such improvements will ensure that this disabled group of people will be fitter and more mobile, will participate in a range of physical activities, will have a wide repertoire of sporting and recreational skills, and through these will be more able to participate fully in society. We shall hear no more gloomy remarks such as the one that stands at the opening of this chapter.

Appendix

Definitions of Conditions Associated With Severe Learning Difficulties

Down's Syndrome: First described in 1866 by Dr John Langdon Down, four types have been identified, all due to chromosomal abnormality. It occurs in approximately 1 in 600 births in the UK and is the largest single cause of mental handicap. Because of distinctive facial features, the condition has been referred to as 'mongolism', a term no longer considered appropriate.

Cerebral Palsy: Evident in early years, it is caused by brain defect, disease or damage. It leads to disorders in movement and posture, sometimes accompanied by mental handicap and sensory impairment. There is a range of severity and types, e.g. spasticity, athetosis and ataxia.

Prader-Willi Syndrome: Obesity, mental handicap, hypotonia and hypogonadism are major features. Motor development is delayed.

Phenylketonuria: Occurring in 1 in 12,000 births in UK, this is a metabolic disorder in which phenylalanine metabolites accumulate in the blood and may lead to mental handicap.

Autism: First described by American psychiatrist Leo Kanner in 1943, autism occurs at all levels of IQ. Boys are more affected than girls (4:1). Where there is mental handicap, brain disease or injury is the probable cause. Some characteristics are failure to relate to people, withdrawal, being 'in a world of their own', anxiety and bizarre, repetitive behaviour such as hand flapping, rocking, jumping.

References

Cambridgeshire County Council. (1987). *'A shared responsibility': Policy guidelines on educational provision for young people with severe learning difficulties.* Cambridge: Author.

Department of Education and Science/Welsh Office. (1984). *The organisation and content of the curriculum: Special schools—A Note by the DES and Welsh Office.* London: Author.

The Education (Handicapped Children) Act. (1970). London: Her Majesty's Stationery Office.

Education, Science & Arts Committee. (1986–87). *Special Educational Needs: Implementation of the Education Act 1981* (3rd Report). London: Her Majesty's Stationery Office.

The Education Reform Act. (1988). London: Her Majesty's Stationery Office.

Gordon, L., Sugden, D., & Fryer, J. (1982). Physical education for children in schools for the educationally subnormal. *Physical Education Review, 2,* 138-145.

Her Majesty's Stationery Office. (1975). *Educating mentally handicapped children*. London: Author.

Physical Education Association (1987). *Physical education in schools* London: Ling.

Statham, J., MacKinnon, D., & Cathcart, H. (1989). *The education fact file*. London: Hodder & Stoughton/Open University Press.

Warnock, H.M. (Chairman) (1978). *Special educational needs. Report of the committee of enquiry into the education of handicapped children and young people*. London: Her Majesty's Stationery Office.

Chapter 8

Examinations and Assessment in Physical Education

Robert Carroll

Never before have teachers and lecturers in schools and colleges been subjected to so much pressure from outside as well as inside the profession to effect changes and innovations to the curriculum, teaching method, assessment, procedures and organization as in recent years. Two of the most important of these changes have been the General Certificate of Secondary Education (GCSE) and Records of Achievement (ROA). In the past, changes in public examinations and assessment procedures have only been peripheral to physical educationalists.

However, the advent of the Certificate of Secondary Education (CSE) brought physical education into the examination orbit and changed the teacher's role (Carroll, 1982). Physical educationalists generally could no longer ignore changes to the examination system, and indeed this major reform to GCSE has stimulated interest in examinations in physical education. At the same time has come the development and interest in 'A' levels in physical education from 6th form and further education colleges, whilst physical education departments in the latter have been moving down examination and vocational paths with City and Guilds (C & G) and Business and Technician Education Council (BTEC) courses in recreation and leisure studies. There too the lecturer has undergone a major change to his or her role (Carroll, 1986).

Records of Achievement or Profiling have been brought in mainly through a dissatisfaction that school leavers, after 5 years of secondary schooling, have only examination certificates to show or, in the case of many pupils, a lack of them. Records of Achievement were to include all achievements and other positive aspects of the pupil, such as social and personality traits. Achievements in physical education and sports, so often commented on by physical education staff and head-teachers when it suited them for public relations or promotion of the school, had rarely seen recognition in official documents, even school reports, nor had personality and social factors, which physical education laid claim to developing. Does this mean that the Department of Education and Science (DES), in 'adopting' ROA, had provided physical education with a heaven-sent opportunity to raise the value of the pupils' achievements and social and personality development in the physical education area and to move physical education from the periphery to a central aspect of the school in the assessment area?

There have been so many simultaneous changes that teachers may be forgiven for either being confused or having misgivings about their introduction. It is the purpose of this paper to try to clarify the situation and allay the misgivings as much as possible by giving a general picture of the present situation regarding examinations and assessment. I will attempt to relate these, where appropriate, to other developments, such as National Curriculum, Technical and Vocational Educational Initiative (TVEI) and health-related fitness (HRF) initiatives. Although examinations and ROA are part of assessment and are closely linked in terms of pupils' achievements and teachers' assessments, the development has taken place separately, and they need to be looked at separately.

Examinations

In 1986 I suggested that we were entering Phase 4 of the examination era in physical education with the advent of GCSE, 'A' level physical education and sport studies, and City and Guilds and BTEC development of the recreation and leisure industries, which physical education and recreation departments had taken on in the further education institutes (Carroll, 1986). Phase 4 has incorporated some of the characteristics of all three previous phases as it has built on existing structures and introduced entirely new examinations. As in Phase 1, Phase 4 has been characterized by establishing and ironing out difficulties of the new examination system (GCSE, 'A' level); at the more individual college level, it has brought in innovation (BTEC recreation and leisure [R and L]). But, as in Phase 2, it has seen a rapid expansion in the numbers of centres and pupils taking the examinations (GCSE, C & G, BTEC). Meanwhile, some consolidation has taken place as in Phase 3, such as the standardization of GCSE from CSE, and 'A' level pilots. Although the development of the different examinations has taken place more or less simultaneously and there has been a general movement towards examinations in the physical education area, the different examinations need to be looked at separately.

General Certificate of Secondary Education

The reform of the examination system, long sought after by many in the teaching profession, was criticized for the timing of its introduction, during a teachers' industrial action. The latter affected the attendance at examination groups' committee meetings and consequently affected the preparation for the new syllabuses. It brought in a general feeling of 'not being quite ready' and having little time for training. For those who had not taught examination pupils before, this played a significant part in deciding whether and when to introduce the GCSE examination in their schools.

Justification for and Organization of the GCSE

From the examination groups' and teacher committees' point of view, it meant there were bound to be difficulties that needed ironing out and syllabus content and assessment that needed refining. This, of course, has brought criticism from teachers who have not always appreciated the difficulties and procedures that have to be gone through. The majority of teachers do not appear to know much about the structure of the examination boards or the procedures for producing syllabuses. They see the boards as independent profit-making bodies and see syllabuses as dominated by administrators. In some regions the physical education teachers' contact with the boards' representatives has not always been satisfactory, due to a number of factors, and has again brought criticism, which reflects on the credibility of physical education as an examination subject. One example of this is that in some regions physical education teachers did not receive the supplementary guidelines along with the syllabus and therefore did not realize that crucial assessment details were missing from athletics and swimming.

Without making excuses for anyone, it is worth pointing out that this has been a particularly difficult time for the examination groups, who, with different constitutions, have had to amalgamate and function as a unit whilst keeping their national and regional functions. For 2 years, they have had to prepare for and introduce the new system whilst continuing with the existing General Certificate of Education (GCE) and CSE, all with the addition of very few extra staff. The four newly created examination groups in England have not all adopted the same structural model and do not function in exactly the same way. This cannot be gone into here, but the different models are shown in Roy, 1986.

However, a main point about the way they function is that subject committees consist of teacher representatives who have devised the new syllabuses, which are then ratified by another committee consisting of experienced teachers in examination work, who oversee and ratify all syllabuses and see that they meet national and subject-specific criteria, and comply with procedures and so on. Teachers who have not sat on subject committees do not appreciate the amount of detail discussed and how long it takes to consider all points of view. These committee members have only a limited amount of time available because they are teachers, having to take time off school to attend the meetings and giving up their own time to prepare for the meetings. A lot of hard work went into the compilation of all the syllabuses.

One of the problems in some regions was that, certainly at first, teachers did not know who their representatives on the committees were or how they were elected. Thus, they did not appear to have representation, and their direct lines of communication were always with an 'anonymous' official at the board. Figure 8.1. shows the Northern Examining Association (NEA) model of representation and functions. Any teacher who wants to attend NEA local advisory group meetings, which function as more than selection mechanisms, should contact his or her regional examination office for dates of meetings.*

---

*See the appendix for names, addresses, and telephone numbers of examining bodies.

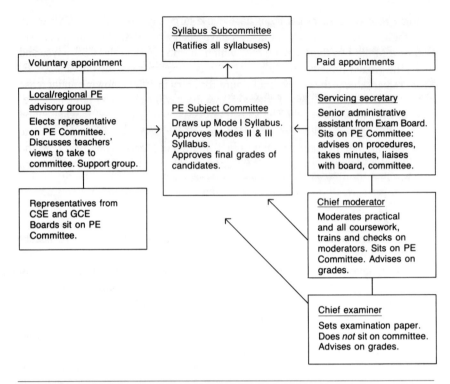

Figure 8.1   NEA model of representation and functions.

Table 8.1 shows the number of candidates for physical education compared to the last available published figures for CSE (Carroll, 1986). The figure for GCSE is for Mode I candidates only, but there are substantial numbers following a Mode II in the Southern Examining Group (SEG) area, so the actual number taking physical education examinations is even larger. As expected, dance and outdoor pursuits/education have become separated from physical education, though it is possible to take dance and outdoor pursuits options in a Mode I physical education syllabus. Dance has its own Mode I or II and is linked to the performing arts in some regions, and it has an entry of approximately 4,000 candidates. Outdoor pursuits has a much smaller entry, insufficient for a Mode I.

Table 8.1   Number of Pupils for GCSE Compared to CSE

| Type of syllabus | Number of pupils examined | | Provisional entry |
	CSE 1985	GCSE 1988 (Mode I only)	GCSE 1989
PE	13,109	18,831	32,700

It can readily be seen that there has been a large increase in the GCSE entry over the CSE figure, which could well have been expected, given the introduction of a Mode I in the NEA region, which did not exist in the CSE days, and given the greater prestige attached to GCSE as it incorporated the previous GCE. More remarkable is the provisional figure for entry in 1989, showing an increase of over 75%. The expectation for 1990 is that there will be a further large increase. This shows a trend away from the idea of physical education as a non-examination subject or one undertaken by a minority of schools and also shows a complete change of attitude by many teachers (see Carroll and MacDonald, 1981). At the same rate of increase, physical education as an examination subject would soon become the norm. Why should there be this change?

Reasons for Change

First, the successes of the CSE in physical education had become more widely known. The fears of examinations, such as the restrictive effect on the curriculum and loss of interest by the pupils, had been replaced by a growing acceptance of the value of examinations in physical education, that is, the increase of knowledge and performance by the pupil and honor for the pupil in a nationally recognized award. Many of the problems of examinations in physical education, for example those of assessment and lack of resources, were seen to be surmountable if not completely solved. Second, the alternative to the examination course was a recreation programme that, though enjoyable to many pupils, was often seen to be repetitive, to lack enough purpose, and perhaps to be increasingly difficult to support in educational circles in an era of increasing accountability, in particular in years when the competition for curriculum time is fierce.

Third, clearly a deciding factor in many cases was the publicity and greater credibility given to the new examination over the CSE because it catered for a wider range of pupils, including the previous GCE high-ability pupils. The effect of providing a Mode I had been seen in some regions in the CSE (Carroll, 1982); this had now been extended to the whole country. In addition, some headteachers wanted the GCSE in physical education, so some staff were forced to consider it, whilst others felt their school could not afford to be left out. But it was not just a case of jumping on the bandwagon: The effects of the market economy on education were clearly being felt. A theory of examination development in physical education based on educational legitimation and acceptance but related to subject and teacher needs and status, outlined in Carroll (1982), are still applicable.

GCSE Syllabuses

Table 8.2 shows the comparative breakdown of the weightings in the assessment of the Mode I schemes. There is a broad agreement on the structure and content of all the examination groups' syllabuses. In addition to the normal 2-year course, the Midland Examining Group (MEG) offers a 1-year mature-students scheme in sport studies with no practical work, whilst NEA approved a 1-year Mode III scheme on the same lines. In the 2-year syllabuses, all go for four or five practical activities worth 50% or 60% of the total marks; they also go for group-ings wherein both team games and individual body-management activities (namely athletics, gymnastics, swimming) have to be assessed. The London and East Anglian Examining Group (LEAG) insists upon the racket sports as a third group, whilst MEG's third group includes racket sports and rounders as well as allowing school submissions of other activities. NEA and SEG also allow submissions of other activities, and NEA and MEG show an extended list of those accepted for 1990 in their new syllabuses. All the schools' major games and popular activities except rounders are included in the NEA and LEAG syllabuses. The NEA physical education subject committee has rejected a submission of rounders from schools on the grounds that the game is not as complex as other games in Group 1. The most popular activities taken by schools in the 1988 examination were, of the games, badminton, soccer, and netball, and in the body-management group, athletics, swimming, and trampolining.

Table 8.2   Assessment Weightings by Percentage of Mode I's in Physical Education

Board	Exam papers	Study	Practical
London and East Anglian Examining Group (LEAG)	20 20		$5 \times 12 = 60$
Northern Examining Association (NEA)	30	20	$4 \times 12.5 = 50$
Midland Examining Group (MEG)	20 30		$5 \times 10 = 50$
Southern Examining Group (SEG) Grades C-F	20 30		$5 \times 10 = 50$
Southern Examining Group (SEG) Ext. grades A+B	14 21 15		$5 \times 10 = 50$
Welsh Joint Examination Committee (WJEC)	12 28		$4 \times 15 = 60$

Note. Numbers represent percentage of the total mark.

All examination groups use continuous assessment for the practical performance, with external moderation and teachers' standardization meetings. However, LEAG divides its 60% of practical performance into 30% as continuous and 30% as final examination. All boards operate very similar criteria based on techniques, skills and tactics where appropriate of the pupils' performance.

MEG's assessment scheme is the most complicated to handle, the assessment sheet columns almost defying teachers' attempts to marry with a fair aggregate mark, causing some difficulties. Moderation of practical work also causes some problems, notably because of the time required to see a number of activities; the timing of the visit at the end of a course or year, when teachers often take a modular approach to teaching; and the need for specialist knowledge in certain activities. These problems have led one board to set up group moderation in an area at one centre and another to rely on teacher standardization rather than the actual visit by a moderator.

On the content of the theory component, there is a large measure of agreement. All boards include what may be termed basic anatomy and physiology and health-related fitness, though section titles may be different. MEG also includes in this section some psychological aspects, often a feature of higher education courses. In a second major theory component, NEA, MEG and SEG go for social aspects, though again under different titles. The NEA calls theirs the organization and participation in physical activities, MEG uses the title 'Contemporary Issues', whilst SEG has 'Sport and Society'. The content of all three is very similar, differing mainly in that NEA and SEG include local and regional participation, a very important topic but one that is difficult to test on in an examination paper because of the variety of answers, due to local and regional variations. LEAG leaves out the social component completely, and as the other theory component does not appear to be wider or taken to any more depth, its is a less broad-based syllabus.

All boards have examination papers (see Table 8.2), but SEG is the only one to go for a differentiated examination paper model. Here Papers 1 and 2 are common, but those candidates wanting to be considered for Grades A or B must take the extended paper of essay-type questions, thus reducing the weighting of the percentage of marks in the first two papers. This is a model that can cause some difficulties in grading, and I would not think it worth adopting for only 15% of the marks and for the top two grades only. LEAG, MEG and SEG have gone for examination papers on the physical activities and sports themselves—questions on the laws, rules, techniques and tactics—but the NEA has not, believing that these are best tested in the practical situation as part of performance. Clearly, it is possible for pupils to know and understand laws, rules, techniques and tactics without necessarily being able to perform well. The NEA has clearly gone for practical performance where these aspects are most valid.

The NEA has perhaps been the most innovative, with its study worth 20% of the assessment. This allows candidates to choose topics of real personal interest from the syllabus and to produce work of their own, even carrying out what can be termed basic research, that is, finding out for themselves or solving a particular problem. This is in line with modern educational ideas, such as TVEI and the GCSE itself. It allows for a wide range of projects relating theory to practical work, for example monitoring fitness in a specific group of people, surveys of pupils' participation in physical activities, organization of competitions, study of local facilities, and analysing training schedules or performances. The pupils may use video recorders, practical work, films and diaries.

The study has met with a mixed reception, partially because some teachers felt projects had got a bad name through misuse in the CSE and partially because a lot of different projects are difficult to handle, the less able pupils finding them tough and needing a lot of guidance. Many teachers had not seen the study as something to be incorporated in curriculum time at first but as something that is left up to the pupil to do in his or her own time. This is now being rectified.

Problems With Introducing the GCSE

Many of the problems physical education teachers faced stemmed from the time scale of the introduction of GCSE, but this was no different for teachers of other subjects. The latter did have the advantage of being 'geared up' to examinations. Because physical education had not been an examination subject in most schools, though, the advantage here was that physical education teachers could wait a year or two before introducing a course; clearly, this is what many teachers have decided to do.

But precisely because physical education had not been an examination subject, the physical education teachers' training and preparation needs were greater. Teachers needed to become more familiar with the theoretical content, depth required and resources available because this was entirely new to the majority of schools, particularly where CSE did not exist. They needed guidance and ideas on how the theoretical and practical work can be linked and not divorced; even in CSE this link was often tenuous. In practical work, which was familiar, they needed to become aware of applying specific criteria and of standards generally and of support in assessment techniques. In the NEA scheme they needed guidance in how to carry out and assess the study and, more generally, the overall curriculum planning for the demands of the whole course.

The Phase 4 training, subject specific, given by the examination groups on a cascade system, was underfunded and woefully inadequate. Being largely 1-day affairs, this training inevitably was superficial and did not even reach all the teachers. LEAG did produce a video on the assessment of three selected practical activities that has been particularly helpful to schools following its scheme. The boards clearly left further training to Local Education Authorities (LEAs), who were usually slow to fill this gap in much-needed service training. Sometimes there was not the expertise in their immediate area, and sometimes there was no specific adviser to organize it. Some LEAs have rectified this now by sending staff on courses or making special arrangements with institutes of higher education.

There has been a serious lack of appropriate resources, for the theory work in particular. Teachers were having to search for information and produce their own material, which can contribute to the success of a course, but both tasks are very time consuming. Many teachers have been grateful to Beashel and Taylor's *Sport Examined* (1986), which has fast become the standard textbook.

The takeup of the syllabuses indicates that there is a general satisfaction with them. Yet, there have been criticisms, and minor adjustments have been made to meet them. One of the strongest criticisms has come from Casbon (1988); it is particularly directed at the MEG syllabus, but many of his points apply more generally. One of his key criticisms is the lack of relationship between the theoretical and practical components. This is suggested by the way the syllabuses are written and is reinforced by the examination questions, some of which would not be out of place in a human biology paper. These questions attempt to get at what children know of the human body, as a basic prerequisite for understanding the relationship between theory and practice, but clearly the knowledge requirement and questions must be very carefully selected.

Part of the problem may lie in the fact that the syllabuses are assessment syllabuses, not teaching syllabuses. There is no reason why the theory work should not be taught in a practical situation related to exercise or physical education. The NEA physical education committee addressed this problem and has a statement to this effect in the syllabus. More attention needs to be paid to this point; perhaps one way to get over it is to replace the examination paper with coursework assignments that ensure the theory-practical link. However, the addition of more coursework for pupils taking a number of subjects will need careful planning because many pupils find they are overburdened either at certain times of the year or in specific subjects.

Other key criticisms by Casbon are that the syllabus is poorly thought out and modern developments were not taken into consideration, which I would dispute. Some of his criticisms can be met by the NEA study, which he fails to acknowledge.

One of the major changes in the revised system is the move to a criterion-referenced examination and the idea of grade-related criteria. Although it is easy enough to write specific criteria for the assessment of specific components of a syllabus, it is not so easy to relate all these criteria to particular grades. The reason for this is that the final grade reached is inevitably a reflection of the aggregate marks for all the components: The way that is reached varies tremendously over the pupil population. The result is a general statement that is not very useful for indicating the level pupils have actually attained, nor for any particular component. It is something that physical education and other subject committees need to address if the idea of grade-related criteria is to be achieved satisfactorily.

The National Curriculum and its related attainment targets have to be used in the examination criterion-referenced system and will be a step towards grade-related criteria. It remains to be seen what will happen with the National Curriculum and assessment targets in physical education.

Perhaps many people feel that the demise of the Mode III's and the standardization of courses have been losses for individuality and staff development. This is a price that physical education and other staff have to pay for acceptance of a more prestigious examination. However, this may be counterbalanced by the growth in the subject at this level. Obviously, standardization and prestige are acceptable to more teachers than individuality and less recognition. However, those teachers who wish to initiate and develop their own courses have plenty of scope in the rest of the school physical education curriculum.

It may or may not be comforting to note that many of the problems are 'start-up' ones that apply equally to other subjects (see Kingdon and Stobart, 1988), but it does mean that these problems should soon be overcome with experience. Indeed, many of them already have been overcome, and there is a great deal more confidence in the examination now than there was 2 years ago. Whilst the remaining difficulties are being sorted out by physical education teachers up and down the country and by the physical education committees, it would be as well to point out that there have been many educational benefits for the pupils, staff development has been widened and enriched, the subject itself has developed, and practical work has been accepted in a prestigious school examination. In short, examinations in physical education have come a long way in a short time, gaining wider acceptance and credibility among non–physical education staff as well as physical education staff.

All subject syllabuses have to be approved by the School Examination and Assessment Council (SEAC, formerly SEC). It has not yet considered the physical education syllabuses. Exactly when it will do so is not known. It is hoped that the syllabuses find favour because certainly there is growing support. However, GCSE will have to fit in with both National Curriculum and ROA, but GCSE may have given a lead to both of these through content, assessment procedures and criterion referencing.

'A' Level: Sport Studies and Physical Education

Francis (1988) has outlined the background and development of 'A' level. There are two 'A' levels in the pilot stage, both under the auspices of the Associated Examining Board (AEB) and both started in September 1986: a Mode I in sport studies, developed mainly by a Sheffield group of teachers; and a Mode II in physical education, developed by groups of teachers in the South. Under the pilot scheme the centres allowed to run examination courses at this level have been carefully vetted and their number restricted whilst an evaluation takes place. Thus, only 24 centres started the sport studies scheme, and a total of 232 candidates were examined in 1988. Meanwhile, because it was accepted a few months later, only 3 of the 15 colleges started on the physical education scheme in 1986, with 34 candidates being examined in 1988; the other 12 started in 1987, and approximately 160 candidates are expected to sit the exam in 1989. Both syllabuses have a core and option programme heavily based in the academic disciplines of anatomy and physiology, biomechanics, psychology, sociology and history. Most of the content is included in degree courses, and the level demanded is high, but this is no different from many other subjects.

There are two main differences between the two syllabuses. The first is that the sport studies scheme has a narrower conception of the physical activities under study, hence its name. However, the wider conception of physical education is not reflected in the number or type of activities in the practical performance in the physical education syllabus. The second difference is that physical education has an assessment of practical performance worth 30%, though in effect it is only half this amount because the rest goes to observation and analysis of performance. I think the types of activities on offer need to be extended and the percentage weighting needs to be considered if it is to retain its different characteristics.

Some of the problems and difficulties of teaching the sport studies syllabus have been raised by Alderson (1988), the AEB chief examiner, and from a survey of participating centres on behalf of the AEB by Wilmut (1988). Some of these apply equally to the physical education scheme, but as yet there is not enough information available, due to the late start by most centres. The strong discipline base affects course cohesion, and the twin demands of depth and breadth over a few disciplines results in a large volume of information and work, which is difficult to cope with. I feel that unless these are looked at, the essential features of sport studies and physical education can be lost.

The strong yet wide discipline base means that there needs to be staff expertise over the sciences and social sciences and staff who can apply the disciplines to sport and physical education. Colleges taking up these courses need to look carefully at their staffing and maybe plan staff development carefully. Perhaps the most serious problem is the lack of resources for this level, which should be rectified. As in the GCSE, teachers have had to do a lot of searching and to produce their own materials, which has been too time consuming. However, it would have been helpful if the known resources could have been related better to the material in the syllabuses. Many of the books listed appear because they are vaguely connected, but the relationships do not always bear close analysis.

To their credit, the AEB has held a number of workshops for staff. These have proved to be most useful, and certainly to be better training than teachers received in the GCSE.

Overall, it appears that the syllabuses have been well received by staff and students. The AEB was happy to recommend to SEAC in 1988 that sport studies should be accepted as a Mode I open to anyone, like other subjects on the 'A' level list. As in the GCSE, many of the problems are teething and establishment ones, which will disappear as staff becomes more familiar with the syllabus and examination requirements and as resources become increasingly available.

The present position is that sport studies is still in its pilot stage but will be resubmitted to SEAC this year (1989) after revisions have taken place. Sixty-five centres, after vetting, were allowed to start teaching the syllabus in 1988 for examination in 1990. Likewise, the number of centres allowed to take the physical education syllabus has been increased; after evaluation and revision, it too will be submitted to SEAC for approval.

If SEAC does accept the revised syllabuses, then the AEB forecasts a rapid expansion in the number of centres and candidates taking up the schemes. At present there is a limited acceptance of the syllabuses for entry to universities and institutes of higher education. For example, the Joint Matriculation Board (JMB) Group does not accept syllabuses whilst they are in the pilot stage (Francis, 1988; Jones, 1988). The acceptance problem is bound to occur with any new examination. The success of the GCSE will stimulate an interest and demand for further study of physical education and sport studies; a rapid expansion in the numbers of pupils will force higher education institutions to think again. The role of the physical education teacher in 6th form colleges will change dramatically when 1-year GCSE and 2-year 'A' level courses are offered.

Vocational Awards—C & G, BTEC

Perhaps the most profound change in the examination field has taken place in colleges of further education, with the movement from physical recreation to vocational training. This development has been outlined by Carroll (1986), and more detailed studies of specific regions have been conducted by Ellingham (1984) and Ryan (1987). It was a natural change in that, like all other college departments catering to the needs of pertinent industries, there was an obvious link between sport and physical recreation and the growth of the recreation and leisure industries. However, it was a huge step to move from merely having a recreative role and servicing function to providing training for industry, even in just the physical recreation and sporting sector.

However, the full range of the recreation and leisure industry is much wider than sport and physical recreation, and the structure is neither homogeneous nor simple. Most of the staff in physical recreation departments were physical education trained, and most had little experience in any industry except teaching, let alone the recreation and leisure industry. There was a serious gap in in-service training, which still exists in most regions. New staff being appointed in FE colleges usually now have to have had experience in the recreation and leisure field. Many institutions of higher education have tried to fill the gap for existing staff by providing in-service training courses with work placement.

The rapid expansion of the recreation and leisure industries in the 1970s, in particular the investment by local authorities and private enterprise in sports and leisure centres, led a small number of colleges to approach the City and Guilds Institute to examine recreation and leisure courses, which subsequently became the C & G 778 syllabus and the later 481 syllabus. From a handful of candidates in the early 1980s the examination has grown each year; more recently there has been a rapid expansion, as shown in Table 8.3. There may well be a leveling off, now that BTEC has developed courses for these industries. The percentage of initial candidates actually going on to gain awards is perhaps startling to many people, but this is partially due to the type of population one gets in colleges of FE: these drops in completion and award rates are quite common.

Structure of the C & G Course

The C & G course is in four levels, each next part progressively more advanced and suited to the levels in the industry: Part I is basic and intended for those enter-

Table 8.3   Number of Candidates for City and Guilds Examinations in 1984 and 1988

City and Guilds Test part number	1984[a]			1988[b]		
	Entries	Completions	Awards	Entries	Completions	Awards
Part I	771	666	449	2,211	1,878	1,323
Part II	416	382	241	2,257	1,934	878
Part III	115	104	31	502	446	160
Part IV	62	58	4	251	NA	130

[a]C & G 778 syllabus. [b]C & G 481 syllabus.

ing the industry. Part II is at an operative technician level, Part III is at supervisory level, and Part IV is for management. Each level has four sections: marketing (services, market factors etc.); provision and control (agencies, activities etc); resource management (laws, maintenance, behaviour etc); and product knowledge (sport and exercise knowledge). The levels are assessed by examinations and coursework set by the City and Guilds Institute, but it is possible to submit individual college courses as long as they meet the criteria, and a few colleges do this.

The strength of the syllabus lies in its structure. It sets out very clearly what the candidate is required to know and do. It is very much a behavioural objectives model. However, it reflects its origins in a sports and physical education background and is very much oriented towards working in sports centres and in sports coaching; an example of this is the inclusion of anatomy and physiology at each level. There seems to be a need to look at the logic and reasons for the inclusion of some of the knowledge to be assessed.

Structure of BTEC

BTEC appears later in the scene for qualifications in the recreation and leisure industries. The difference between C & G and BTEC is that the former is an examining body, whilst the latter is a validating one. BTEC schemes are college-devised schemes within carefully drawn up national guidelines and are moderated by BTEC-appointed moderators.

There are 4 levels of BTEC qualification.

1. BTEC First Certificates and Diplomas are initial qualifications for an industry. They would be regarded as satisfying the former GCE 'O' level and presumably the equivalent in GCSE.
2. BTEC National Certificates and Diplomas are recognized as qualifications for technicians or junior administrators. They are readily accepted as equivalent to 'A' levels.
3. BTEC Higher National Certificates and Diplomas are for higher grade technician, supervisory and managerial levels.
4. BTEC Continuing Education Certificates and Diplomas are for adults with at least 3 years experience in the industry and are for management levels.

In all these levels the difference between a certificate and a diploma is dependent on the length of study.

BTECs have core units, are common to many industries and are often taken by staff in business studies departments. They include other core units in the leisure industry; e.g. at national level, there are two core units, covering (a) the leisure industry and (b) marketing leisure services. There are a number of optional units covering seven identified sectors of the industry: arts and entertainment, sport and recreation, tourism, countryside, cultural recreation, hospitality, parks and amenities, and horticulture. The width of the offerings at the different levels is too great to go into here, and the individual nature of the college development, combined with the fact that it is such a recent development, means there is not as yet a complete picture of exactly what is happening within BTEC development. There is now a great deal of interest in BTEC leisure courses, and a rapid expansion is forecast (see Table 8.4).

Table 8.4   Number of Registrations for BTEC Awards in 1987-88

BTEC category	Level	Males	Females	Total
Leisure studies	FC+D^a	259	239	498
	NC+D^b	789	580	1,369
	HNC+D^c	69	81	150
	CED^d	10	3	13
Leisure management	CEC+D^e	31	16	47

^{a}First Certificates & Diplomas. ^{b}National Certificates & Diplomas. ^{c}Higher National Certificates & Diplomas. ^{d}Continuing Education Diplomas. ^{e}Continuing Education Certificates & Diplomas.

Continuing Evolution of C & G and BTEC

We are certain to see more change to C & G and BTEC syllabuses, and to the structure of courses leading to qualifications in recreation and leisure, because of the establishment of the National Council for Vocational Qualifications (NCVQ) in 1986 and the advent of Training and Enterprise Councils (TECs). The NCVQ was set up by the government to bring some order to vocational qualifications and to set the national standards. NCVQ therefore gives its seal of approval to the courses of other bodies, such as C & G and BTEC, in an area of work (such as engineering, catering, leisure) at specific levels of achievement. There should thus be an easily understandable framework that will make clear paths of progression in an industry. This is something C & G and BTEC had clearly tried to do with their levels. However, judging by those areas of work that have already received the NCVQ hallmark (e.g. C & G catering), the recreation and leisure syllabuses will have to become more job specific and give more on-the-job training as part of a unit accreditation system. A new framework for recreation and leisure syllabuses for both C & G and BTEC will be going to NCVQ in May 1989, so by the time this study is published, the new framework may well be approved.

The other influential agents of change may well be TECs, which are advisory bodies set up by the government in March 1989. They consist of representatives of local industries chosen to oversee college courses in relation to local needs. They are just now being founded by local chambers of commerce, so it is difficult to know the extent of their influence yet. There are expected to be about 100 TECs nationally over the next 3 years. The relationship between TECs and the regional advisory councils, which are education based, is not known. Whether there will be a conflict between local and national industry needs is not certain, but the provision of recreation and leisure facilities and the needs of the industry are similar in different regions.

Clearly, there has been a dramatic change in direction in physical education in many schools from the 4th year and above and in FE establishments. This change in direction affects the 'classification and framing' (see Bernstein, 1972), that is, the structure and boundaries of the subject and the processes of teaching and learning. There is a change in the ideological base and subject knowledge, which affects both the teachers' and pupils' roles and the departmental status and function within the school. Table 8.5 summarizes those changes, but it must be remembered that traditional ideologies and roles exist simultaneously with non-examination physical education.

Records of Achievement and Profiling

The position with ROA and profiling is much less clear than with examinations. The terms *ROA* and *profile* are usually used interchangeably and cover a wide range of methods for recording and reporting pupils' achievements. They include more than a record of actual achievements within subjects, taking in personal qualities and evaluative comments. They can be both formative and summative. ROAs include pupil as well as teacher recording and often a joint, negotiated effort between teacher and pupil. The types and variety of ROA are enormous because of the way they have been left to develop, including individually developed school records, even idiosyncratic subject ones, LEA-developed schemes, and recognized schemes by examining bodies such as Northern Partnership Records of Achievement (NPRA) and South East Records of Achievement (SERA) in conjunction with schools and LEAs.

The original purpose of ROA was to provide information about non-examination pupils. Early schemes, such as Swindon Records of Personal Achievement in 1969 (Swales, 1979) and the Evesham checklist in 1979, smacked of low status (Fairbairn, 1988). In 1981 a Schools Council Survey indicated that there were 25 schools using profile reports (Balogh, 1982). The Oxford Delegacy of Local Examinations took the initiative with a profile of three components: students' attainments and experiences, achievements within the curriculum in the main subjects, and a record of examination results. Some four LEAs and 40 schools took this up within the next 2 years (Fairbairn, 1988).

The DES (1984) expressed its concern about school leavers—that is, all school leavers (not just non-examination pupils)—departing school without adequate records of what they had achieved.

> Records and recording systems should recognise, acknowledge and give credit for what pupils have achieved and experienced, and not just in terms of public examinations but in other ways as well. . . . by the end of the decade to establish throughout England and Wales arrangements by which all young people

Table 8.5   Changes in Direction on the Introduction of Examinations in Physical Education Departments in Schools and Colleges

	Changes in GCSE 'A' level		Changes in C & G, BTEC	
	From Recreational	To Educational	From Recreational	To Vocational
Ideological base				
Knowledge base	Practical (knowing how)	Practical and theoretical (how and what)	Practical (knowing how, physical experience)	Theoretical and job related (knowing how and what, job experience)
	Narrow (activity related)	Broad (activities and extension to sciences and social sciences)	Narrow (activity related)	Broad (recreation and leisure industries)
Level criteria	Participation: physical	Performance: physical and academic	Participation: physical	Performance: academic and vocational
Role of teacher	Recreationalist, supervisor, official	Educationalist, teacher, coach Assessor, examiner	Recreationalist, supervisor, official	Vocational, trainer, educationalist Assessor, examiner
Department status	Marginal	Central	Marginal	Central
Department function	Supporting value system	Transmitting knowledge, skills, values, and selective mechanism	Servicing other departments	Vocational training and selective mechanism

in secondary schools will have a record of achievement and will take with them, when they leave school. (p. 4)

This was to be a summary document prepared within a national framework but leaving scope for local variation.

Both the Schools Council and the DES funded pilot schemes in selected LEAs (see DES, 1988). Some schools have worked on ROA unfunded, but it is only now that the majority of teachers are getting to grips with ROA, as a result of DES policy.

Physical Educators' Problems With ROA

Most of the problems physical education teachers face with ROA have been no different from those of other teachers. All teachers have to grapple with this new initiative, and it is not as simple as it sounds to implement. If a profile of a pupil is to be really useful, it has to be comprehensive, including a wide range of all possible achievements and personal attributes. It is much easier to decide which achievements to include and much easier to assess, in the context of a subject, pertinent base criteria than it is to decide which personal attributes are required and to assess them. Clearly, what to select cannot be divorced from the purpose of the records. From the DES statements it is clearly meant for employers, for further education, for 'personal development and progress by improving their motivation', and also for schools themselves to evaluate their curriculum.

Therefore ROA have to serve several purposes at the same time. They clearly have to be an integral part of the educational process, a document that is formative yet serving as a summative record that will be used as a selective mechanism by employers and further education. In this respect, it shares the same function as the GCSE. As it has been very much an individual school development model within very general guidelines, the selection of criteria, achievements and attributes and the format and presentation of the record have placed an enormous demand upon teacher time and resources, very often with little or no training.

Physical education teachers are not used to formal assessments; most of their evidence is fleeting, ephemeral performances rather than a permanent presentation, as in classroom writing; and most of their comments or reports relate to ability and effort (Carroll, 1976). The lack of hard evidence means the teacher has to place a lot of reliance on his or her perception and observation—in a context where very often a lot is going on at the same time with a lot of pupils, e.g. in games—and then on his or her memory and ability to relate to other occasions of a similar nature. This is often very different from classrooms, where the context and situation are much simpler. In the sports milieu personal qualities and effort are often inextricably linked with achievement.

Physical education teachers are just learning to extrapolate the technical skills and decision making from the personal qualities in criteria laid down within GCSE. ROA are an opportunity to emphasize the positive aspects of the personal qualities, something physical education teachers have often seen as one of their objectives (see Kane, 1974, and Underwood, 1983). However, many physical education teachers will feel a little uneasy here without more experience, and great care must be taken in fairness to the pupil.

Individual Nature of ROA

Two of the new aspects of ROA are pupil self-assessment and negotiation between teacher and pupil. Not all schools have included these aspects in the pilot scheme (DES, 1988), but it is something that appears to be growing. These aspects place an extra burden on time. Physical education teachers nearly always mention time as a factor in assessment (e.g. Brook, 1986, and Booton, 1986). It may well be easier for staff whose main teaching takes place in a classroom to arrange interviews and negotiating time with pupils than for physical education teachers, who teach in gymnasia, sports halls and playing fields. Some form of team teaching or extra staffing may well be required to conduct these initiatives satisfactorily.

Because of the individual nature of the development of ROA, it is difficult to get a clear picture of exactly what is going on, how much has gone on, and whether there are similarities and common factors, criteria or presentation. Although many writers stress the need for individuality (e.g. Booton, 1986, and Skelthorne, 1986), many teachers gain from what is going on elsewhere. They can extract what is good practice in other schools and possibly learn from other teachers' mistakes, preventing them from making the same ones.

I have seen one or two examples of presentation of ROA in physical education that show great ingenuity, look interesting for pupils and staff, and have led the way in the school for other departments to follow. This will do nothing but good for physical education. Hopefully, it will help gain acceptance of physical education achievements as valuable in the inevitable hierarchy of educational achievements and the status game (see Goldstein and Nuttall, 1986). I have come across record books that have other information in them for the pupil (e.g. knowledge about sports, quizzes, amusing quotes) that makes them especially interesting and perhaps help the pupil retain motivation—and their records. However, the majority of ROA are a lot more straightforward. It is quite common to use banks of statements, which saves the teacher a lot of time, and some have been computerized for efficiency (Skinsley, 1986).

Structure of ROA

It seems to be quite common to have a sheet for each activity. On it are places for the pupil and/or the teacher to record the achievements based on technique and skill criteria. They mark either a simple tick if the skill is achieved, or rate the knowledge or skill on a 5-point scale (as in Table 8.6). There may be from 10 to 20 statements to assess.

Such records give the physical education teacher an idea of the pupil's skills and at what levels of competency. These sheets are often supplemented by state-

Table 8.6   A Skill-Criteria ROA to be Filled in by the Pupil

Unit/module: Badminton	1	2	3	4	5
1. I use the correct grip on the racket.					
2. I can serve the shuttle high.					
3. I am able to clear the shuttle the full length of the court.					
4. I know the rules of badminton.					
5. I can umpire a game of badminton.					
[So on]					

1 = Low/Poor   5 = High/Very good

ments on such personal qualities as behaviour in lessons, attitude to the activity, attendance and punctuality in lessons and extracurricular activities, effort, bringing kit, concentration, carrying out instructions and tasks, working with other people, personal fitness and using initiative. Clearly, some of these qualities can be linked to developments within TVEI, personal and social development programmes and residential experience.

Of the attributes mentioned, testing physical fitness is of interest but still a little controversial. It has an objectiveness that is appealing for ROA, but Fox and Biddle (1988) warn of the dangers and limitations of the tests. All these attributes give the physical education teacher knowledge about how the pupil carries out those skills already recorded. Sometimes there are places on the sheets for further comments, which can result in lengthy ROA over a period of time. Therefore, there is often a summary sheet, which may be little more than the much-maligned school report but is usually more detailed.

The complete ROA is a big improvement on the school report because the teacher has much more recorded detailed knowledge of each pupil. And therein lies the crunch: The time taken to observe the pupils carefully and to negotiate assessments is a headache for physical education teachers. They must not let the 'tail wag the dog'. As the DES evaluation report states, 'Effective ROA schemes will not be cheap: Cheap ROA schemes will not be effective' (DES, 1988).

Quality Control of ROA

The latest statement from the DES is the *Report of the ROA National Steering Committee* (1989b). It recommends quality control and procedures for validation, accreditation, verification and authentication of ROA. It also puts forward draft guidelines under three headings: aims and objectives, criteria for the accreditation of processes, and principles and requirements for the format and content of summary documents.

Of particular interest to physical education teachers is the mention that out-of-school sporting achievements, personal qualities, and teachers' assessments should always be supported by contextual evidence. Therefore, teachers have to use banks of statements with more care. There is also a statement on resource implications from the pilot schemes, and this includes staff time as well as financial costs. The committee recommends that all schools should be expected to conform to national guidelines for the autumn term of 1990. This, I feel, is a very welcome document in that it sets out draft guidelines and standardization for ROA, which were in danger of becoming too varied and losing their coherence and structure, which may have reflected poorly on their credibility.

ROA in FE Colleges

ROA have been going on in colleges of FE, too. The latest situation here is that the National Record Of Vocational Achievements will be extended to include as many people as possible who are working to NCVQs in a credit accumulation scheme. Clearly, these are going to be very useful to employers as selective mechanisms and in determining training needs.

Conclusion

Perhaps the question that now needs to be addressed is how developments in examinations and ROA fit in with such other government initiatives as TVEI and the National Curriculum and subject testing. It is clear there is a link between TVEI and both examinations and ROA. First, part of TVEI is employment orientated. ROA are employment orientated in that one of their main functions is to serve employers. TVEI is the first stage, along with parallel developments such as the Certificate of Pre-Vocational Education (CPVE), in vocational training and qualifications. Second, TVEI has an educational orientation, linked to ROA through qualities and achievements on a profile system and linked to GCSE through developing ideas in teaching and learning and the curriculum. TVEI has, in fact, provided the money to many schools for carrying out many of the ideas related to HRF and fitness testing, the funds taking care of technology, equipment, and expensive activities such as residential outdoor pursuits courses. Both of these examples can be part of GCSE or the non-examination curriculum.

At the time of this writing, it is not certain how the National Curriculum and subject testing will affect physical education. The position is that a subject working group will be set up by the DES to consider the National Curriculum and testing; this is expected to occur in the summer of 1990. It is clearly going to be some time later that the group sets out its proposals for consultation; according to DES, the first unreported assessment will take place in the summer of 1994 (see DES, 1989a, Annex C2, for timetable).

There is no reason why GCSE and ROA cannot fit into those requirements as they will do in other subjects. In fact, criteria laid down in GCSE and ROA based on an 'experiences model' can give a lead in those requirements.

Appendix

Examining Bodies

GCSE

London and East Anglian Examining Group (LEAG)
"The Lindens"
Lexden Road
Colchester CO3 3RL

Tel: Colchester (0206) 549594

Physical education—GCSE
Dance—GCSE (syllabuses £0.75 each)

Midland Examining Group (MEG)
c/o West Midlands Examinations Board
Norfolk House
Smallbrook Queensway
Birmingham B5 4NJ

Tel: 021 6312151

The theory and practice of physical education—GCSE
Dance—GCSE (syllabuses £0.60 each)

Northern Examining Association (NEA)
c/o YREB
Scarsdale House
136 Derbyshire Land
Sheffield S8 8SE

Tel: 0742 557436

Southern Examining Group (SEG)
c/o South East Regional Examinations Board
Beloe House
2/10 Mount Ephraim Road
Royal Tunbridge Wells
Kent TN1 1EU

Tel: Tunbridge Wells (0892) 35311

Physical education—GCSE
Dance—GCSE (syllabuses £1.00 each)

Welsh Joint Examination Committee (WJEC)
245 Western Avenue
Cardiff CF5 2YX

Tel: Cardiff (0222) 561231

Physical education—GCSE (syllabus £0.75)
  Paper 1 Dance or Gymnastics
  Papers 2 and 3 compulsory (specimen papers £0.20 each)

'A' Level

Associated Examining Board (AEB)
Stag Hill House
Guildford
Surrey GU2 5XJ

Tel: Guildford (0483) 506506

Sport studies—'A' level
Physical education—'A' level

Vocational Qualifications

City and Guilds of London Institute (C & G)
46 Britannia Street
London WC1X 9RG

Tel: 01 278 2468

Certificate in recreation and leisure studies (481)

Business and Technician Education Council (BTEC)
Central House
Upper Woburn Place
London EC1H OHH

Tel: 01 388 3288

Leisure studies—BTEC First, National and Higher National Certificate/Diploma
  Courses

References

Alderson, J. (1988). *Issues and strategies: 'A' level national conference for 'A' level physical education and sport studies*. Guildford: Associated Examining Board.

Balogh, J. (1982). *Profile reports for school leavers*. London: Longman.

Beashel, P., & Taylor, J. (1986). *Sport examined*. London: Macmillan.

Bernstein, B. (1972). On the classification and framing of educational knowledge. In M.F.D. Young (Ed.), *Knowledge and Control* (pp. 47-69). London: Collier Macmillan.

Booton, P. (1986). One form of assessment. *Bulletin of Physical Education, 22*, 32-42.

Brook, S. (1986). *Teachers' perceptions of pupil assessment in physical education.* Unpublished master's thesis, University of Manchester, Manchester.

Carroll, R. (1976). Physical education teachers' own evaluation of their lessons. *Journal of Psychological and Social Aspects of Human Movement,* (Occasional Paper No. 2), 30-39.

Carroll, R. (1982). Examinations and curriculum change in physical education. *Physical Education Review,* **5**, 26-36.

Carroll, R. (1986). Examinations in physical education: An analysis of trends and developments: In The Management Committee (Ed.), *Trends and developments in physical education: Conference papers of the VIII Commonwealth and International Conference on Sport, Physical Education, Dance, Recreation and Health* (pp. 233-239). London: E. & F.N. Spon.

Carroll, R., & MacDonald, A.I. (1981). Male physical education teachers' opinions about physical education examinations in schools. *Bulletin of Physical Education,* **17**, 23-30.

Casbon, C. (1988). Examinations in physical education a path to curriculum development. *British Journal of Physical Education,* **19**, 217-219.

Department of Education and Science. (1984). *Records of achievement: A statement of policy.* London: Her Majesty's Stationery Office.

Department of Education and Science. (1988). *Developments in records of achievement 1986-88.* London: Author.

Department of Education and Science. (1989a). *National Curriculum: From policy to practice.* London: Author.

Department of Education and Science. (1989b). *Records of achievement: Report of the R.O.A. National Steering Committee.* London: Her Majesty's Stationery Office.

Ellingham, K. (1984). *Development of physical education and recreation in selected colleges of further education.* Unpublished master's thesis, University of Manchester, Manchester.

Fairbairn, D.J. (1988). Pupil profiling: New approaches to recording and reporting achievement. In R. Murphy & H. Torrance (Eds.), *The changing face of educational assessment* (pp. 35-66). Milton Keynes: Open University Press.

Fox, K., & Biddle, S. (1986). Health related fitness testing in schools. *Bulletin of Physical Education,* **22**, 54-64.

Francis, J. (1988). Examinations at 'A' level G.C.E. in physical education and sport studies: The current situation. *British Journal of Physical Education,* **19**, 212-213.

Goldstein, H., & Nuttall, D. (1986). Can graded assessments, records of achievement and modular assessment co-exist with G.C.S.E.? In C.V. Gipps (Ed.), *The G.C.S.E.: An uncommon examination* (Bedford May Papers No. 29, pp. 55-66). London: London Institute of Education.

Jones, T. (1988). The 'A' levels as qualifications for entry into higher education. In *Report of a National Conference for 'A' level physical education and sport studies* (pp. 16-17). Guildford: Associated Examining Board.

Kane, J.E. (1974). *Physical education in secondary schools.* London: Macmillan.

Kingdon, M., & Stobart, G. (1988). *G.C.S.E. examined.* London: Falmer Press.

Roy, W. (1986). *The new examination system*. London: Croom Helm.

Ryan, B. (1987). Curriculum innovation in physical education in further education in the Eastern Region. Unpublished master's thesis, University of Manchester, Manchester.

Skelthorne, A. (1986). The development of a profiling system. *Bulletin of Physical Education, 22*, 143-147.

Skinsley, M. (1986). Profiling using the computer. *Bulletin of Physical Education, 22*, 48-51.

Swales, T. (1979). *Record of personal achievement: An independent evaluation of the Swindon R.P.A. Scheme*. (Pamphlet 16). London: Schools Council.

Underwood, C.L. (1983). *The physical education curriculum in the secondary school: Planning and implementation*. London: Falmer Press.

Wilmut, J. (1988). *An evaluation of the 2nd year of the course in sport studies at advanced level*. Guildford: Associated Examining Board.

Index

A

Academic performance, and physical education, 28-29
Active Lifestyles Project, 70, 90
Activity independence, 13
Adapted games, 127
Adventure activities, 47
'A' level examinations in physical education, 146-147
Associated Examining Board, 146-147
Athletic sports, 45-46

B

Body Owner's Manual, The, 24
Bogalusa Heart Study, 23
British Council of Physical Education, 76
Business and Technical Education Council
    continuing evolution of syllabuses for, 150-151
    structure of courses, 149-150

C

Cardiorespiratory fitness, and coronary prevention, 12
Cardiovascular disease
    occupational activity studies, 1-2
    physical education preventing risk factors for, 22-23
    programmes to reduce risk factors among primary school children, 25-26
    relationship with physical activity, 1-4
Central Council for Physical Recreation, Sports Leadership Award, 50
Certificate of Pre-Vocational Education, 156
Children with severe learning difficulties
    advantages of integration for, 129
    agencies contributing to physical education for, 129-130, 133
    characteristics of, 121-122
    current practices for, 124-130
    definitions of conditions of, 134
    improving physical education for, 130-133
    increased resources needed by, 132-133
    integration of, 123-124, 129
    legislation affecting education of, 123
    need for specialist teachers for, 132
    options for, 124-125
    physical education curriculum provided for, 125-129
    physical education in total education of, 130-133

physical education needs of, 125, 126-127
    in special schools, 124-127
    survey of curriculum content for, 127-129
    training teachers for, 131-132
City and Guilds
    continuing evolution of syllabuses for, 150-151
    number of candidates for, 148
    structure of courses, 148-149
Coeducational programmes
    boys gaining more from, 108
    detracting from girls' educational performance, 107-108
    not automatically conferring equality of opportunity, 107-109
Community involvement in physical activity of children, 9
Community Sports Leaders Awards Scheme, 68
Competition, options for handling in games teaching, 96
Conditioning activities, 47
Coronary heart disease. *See* Cardiovascular disease
Coronary Prevention in Children Project, 6, 9
Court games, 46
Curriculum
    not keeping pace with developments, 37-38
    traditional model, 37

D

Dance
    problems with teaching, 49
    as sport, 48
    as a valued cultural form, 48-49
Discrimination
    confronting, 116-117
    resulting from gatekeeping, 116

E

Education, purpose of, 43-44
Education (Handicapped Children) Act of 1970, 123
Education Act of 1971, 123
Education Reform Act of 1988, 40, 63, 72, 130
Egalitarianism, 104-105
English Schools Football Association, 89
Equal access, confused with equal opportunity, 105-106, 107

Equality
  egalitarianism as an interpretation of,
    104-105
  equal opportunity as an interpretation of,
    105-109
  flaws in concept of equal treatment,
    102-103
  unacceptability of equal outcomes approach
    to, 103-104
Equal opportunity
  achieving, 109
  and coeducational physical education,
    107-109
  confronting discrimination, 116-117
  confused with equal access, 105-106, 107
  dimensions of change needed for, 110-111
  in education, 105-109
  myths affecting nonparticipation, 106-107
  not automatically conferred by
    coeducational programmes, 107-109
  and physical education, 101-118
  preconditions affecting, 106
  and professionalism, 113-114
  stages of problem solving applied to,
    109-110
  training needed to effect, 113
Equal outcomes, unacceptability of, 103-104
Equal treatment, impossibility of, 102-103
Exercise programmes
  in addition to normal school curricula,
    26-28
  Superkids-Superfit, 26
Extracurricular activities
  extracurricular games, 33, 88-91
  need for cooperation in providing, 60
  options for managing, 89-91
  responsibility for, at the secondary level,
    86-87
  teacher's roles in, 89

F
Family involvement in physical activity of
  children, 9-10
Field games, 46
Fighting games, 46
Fitness testing, problems with, 11-12, 155

G
Games
  for children with severe learning
    disabilities, 127, 128
  court, 46
  extracurricular, 88-91
  field, 46
  fighting, 46
  importance of, 79
  improving training for using, 84-85
  inadequate teaching of, 80-81
  innings, 46
  net, 46
  new, 47-48
  new directions in teaching, 79-98
  in the physical education curriculum, 91-92
  in the primary sector, 82-85
  role in physical education programme,
    79-88
  roles of teachers and coaches in, 81-82,
    88, 89
  target, 44-45
  teaching for understanding approach to,
    91-95
  uses of, 79
Games education
  classification system to develop curriculum,
    95-96
  encouraging skill development, 96-97
  need for coherent approach, 87-88
  presenting competitive options, 96
  role of National Curriculum in improving,
    97-98
  shared principles, 95
Game sports, 46-47
Gatekeeping, in physical education, 115-116
  discrimination resulting from, 116
General Certificate of Secondary Education
  advantages of, compared with Certificate
    of Secondary Education, 141
  criticism of syllabuses for, 144-145
  justification for and organization of,
    139-141
  and National Curriculum, 145
  number of candidates for, 140-141
  problems with introducing, 144-146
  status of physical education, 60, 137
  structure and content of examination
    groups' syllabuses for, 141-143
  teacher preparation inadequate for, 144
  variations in syllabuses for, 141-143
Generic sport activity experience in physical
  education curriculum, 55-57
Go for Health project, The, 25
Gymnastic sports, 45

H
Happy Heart Project, 29-33
Health
  contribution of physical education to, 49-50
  as an objective of physical education,
    17-18, 20-21, 23-29
  promoted by physical activity, 32-33
  promoting, in primary school physical
    education, 21-23
  reservations about role of physical education
    in promoting, 18-21
Health and Physical Education Project, The
  20, 21
Health education
  overlap with physical education, 19-20
  in physical education curriculum, 59
Health Education Authority, 126-127
Health-Related Behavior Questionnaire, 11

Health-related fitness for children with
    severe learning disabilities, 128-129
Healthy lifestyles
    education to promote, 19
    encouraged by physical education, 22
    need for physical activity to promote,
        10, 19
Heart Smart programme, 25-26
Higher education role in training for
    physical activity of children, 13
Human studies, 113

I

Inner London Education Authority report,
    71, 83, 85, 88
Innings games, 46
Integration model for physical education/
    sport interface, 71-76
    assumptions of, 72
    changes needed for effective functioning
        of, 75-76
International Centre for Information and
    Study of Special Needs Education,
    131-132

K

Know Your Body programme, 24-25

L

Lawn Tennis Association, 87
Leisure education
    for children with severe learning
        disabilities, 127, 130
    in physical education curriculum, 42, 59
    role of sports participation in, 70
London and East Anglian Examining
    Group, 142-143

M

Media role in sport consumption, 50-51
Midland Examining Group, 141-143
Motor skill development for children with
    severe learning disabilities, 127, 128
Movement mastery, 55, 56, 73
My Favorite Subject, 71, 84, 90

N

National Coaching Foundation, 50, 68,
    76, 86
National Council for Vocational
    Qualifications, 150
National Curriculum. *See also* Curriculum;
    Physical education curriculum
    allocation for physical education, 30
    cross-curricular potential of, 68, 75
    framework for multidisciplinary approach
        provided by, 10
    and games education, 97-98
    issues facing physical education in, 38-43
    physical education as a foundation subject
        in, 59-60, 63
    rationale for physical education in, 43-54
    reasons for, 38

and subject testing, 156
National School Sports Association, 73
Net games, 46
New games, 47-48
Northern Examining Association, 139-143

O

Occupational activity studies, 2
Organized competitive activities, 45-47

P

Physical activity. *See also* Physical edu-
    cation
    in addition to normal school curricula,
        26-28
    as an aspect of healthy lifestyles, 10
    changing children's attitudes towards, 10
    choosing appropriate motivation for, 12-13
    community attitudes important to, 9
    demonstrated need for, 2-3
    effect of daily physical education on, 27-28
    equipment used for monitoring, 5-6
    family involvement important to, 9-10
    implications for children's physical
        education, 9-13
    implications for teacher preparation, 13
    importance of, 17
    importance of activity independence in, 13
    link to coronary heart disease, 1-4
    low levels of, among children, 8-9
    need for awareness of importance of, 9
    primary and secondary school children's,
        compared, 8
    problems with fitness testing during, 11-12
    promoted by physical education, 11
    promoting health, 32-33
    reasons for promoting, in schools, 18-19
    recommendations for, 4
    school involvement in, 10-13
    sex-steryotyping a problem with, 9-10
    studies of, 4-9
Physical education. *See also* Physical
    activity
    and academic performance, 28-29
    aims of, 44, 54-55
    'A' level examinations in, 146-147
    and benefits of daily activity, 27-28
    children discouraged by, 11
    for children with severe learning
        difficulties. *See* Children with
        severe learning difficulties
    City and Guilds courses in, 148-149
    coeducational programmes, 107-109
    confronting discrimination in, 116-117
    confused with sport, 64-65. *See also*
        Physical education/sport interface
    contributing to health, 22, 49-50
    dance and sport as valued cultural forms
        in, 44-49
    developing a total concept of, 28-29
    and equal opportunities, 101-118

Physical education (*continued*)
  examinations in, 137, 138-151
  examining bodies in, 157-158
  extracurricular programme in, 60
  as a foundation subject in the National
      Curriculum, 59-60, 63
  gatekeeping in, 115-116
  'gendering' of, 113-114
  general benefits from, 28-29
  as a General Certificate of Secondary
      Education subject, 60, 138-146
  health as an objective of, 17-18, 20-21
  health education overlapping with, 19-20
  health-related fitness as part of, 11
  healthy lifestyles promoted by, 18-19, 22
  imbalance in, 11
  integrating children with severe learning
      disabilities, 123-124, 129
  interface with sport. *See* Physical education/
      sport interface
  lack of interest in, 39
  for leisure, 42, 59, 70, 127, 130
  need for curricular changes in, 11
  objectives for, 55
  preventing cardiovascular disease risk
      factors, 22-23
  in primary schools. *See* Primary school
      physical education
  professionalism in, 111-115
  records of achievement and profiling,
      137-138, 151-156
  related human studies undervalued in, 113
  reservations about, role in health promotion,
      18-21
  role in sport consumption, 51
  scholarship associated with, 53
  in secondary schools. *See* Secondary school
      physical education
  sport as a vehicle for, 67
  topics covered by, 19
  value of habitual physical activity promoted
      by, 22
  vocational awards, 147-151
  vocational preparation not adequately
      covered by, 70
  women lacking parity in profession of,
      114
Physical Education Advisory Group, 76
Physical Education Association, 11, 109,
    112, 126, 131
Physical education curriculum. *See also*
    National Curriculum
  for 'A' level, 146-147
  balance needed in, 53-54, 80
  for Business and Technical Education
      Council qualification, 149-151
  causes of problems in, 39
  challenges to traditional interpretation,
      41
  for children with severe learning
      difficulties, 125-129

City and Guilds courses, 148-149
  components of, 10
  conceptual clarity lacking in, 38-39
  cooperation with other areas needed in,
      54
  games experience in, 91-92
  for General Certificate of Secondary
      Education, 141-143, 144-146
  generic sport activity experience phase
      in, 55-57
  importance of, 43
  leisure opportunities as a concern for, 42
  mastery of movement phase in, 55, 56
  National Curriculum debate offering
      opportunities for, 39, 40, 43
  optional 4th/5th year, 59-60
  performance expectations for, 40
  physical education for life phase, 59
  place of sport in, 39
  range of sport activity experience phase,
      57-59
  role in preparation for life, 42
  roots of subject not adequately investigated
      for, 40-42
  scholarship needed in, 52-53
  skillful performance not meaningful to, 41
  stages of progression not identified for,
      40
  stages proposed for, 55-59
  teaching of morality not appropriate for, 41
Physical education for life phase in physical
    education curriculum, 59
Physical education/sport interface, 63-76
  integration model for, 71-76
  reinforcement model for, 67-69
  sequence model for, 69-71
  substitution model for, 64-66
  versus model for, 66-67
Physical education teachers
  'licensing' causing concern, 65
  inadequate training of, for primary
      sector, 82
  role in games education, 87, 88, 89
Physical fitness assessment problems, 11-12
Primary school physical education
  Happy Heart Project and, 29-33
  health promotion important in, 21-23
  helping students achieve in sport, 72-73
  integrated heart health programmes in,
      24-26
  primary teachers inadequately trained for,
      82-84
  programmes in addition to normal school
      curricula, 26-29
  review of initiatives emphasizing health
      in, 23-29
Problem solving stages, 109-110
Professionalism, 111-115
  challenges to, 112
  confronting discrimination in, 116-117
  dangers of, 114-115

and establishing equality of opportunity, 113-114
ethical dimensions of, 111-112
and gender-restrictive practices, 114
and implicit expectation of standards, 111-112
and widening knowledge gap, 115

R

Records of Achievement and Profiling, 137-138, 151-156
in further education colleges, 156
individual nature of, 154
physical educator's problems with, 153-154
pupil self-assessment in, 154
purposes of, 137-138, 151, 153
quality control of, 155-156
structure of, 154-155
time as a factor in assessment of, 154
types and variety of, 151
Reinforcement model for physical education/ sport interface, 67-69
Report of the ROA National Steering Committee, 155-156

S

School Examination and Assessment Council, 146-147
School involvement in physical activity of children, 10-13
School Sport Forum, 10, 43-45, 85, 86
Science in the National Curriculum, 10
Secondary school physical education
extracurricular opportunities, 86-87
facilitating achievement in sport, 73-74
need for coherent games education, 87-88
partnerships needed in games teaching, 85-86
Sequence model for physical education/ sport interface, 69-71
Sex-stereotyping of physical activity of children, 9-10
Short Tennis Leaders Award, 87
Snoezelen, for children with severe learning disabilities, 129
Southern Examining Group, 142-143
Sport
adventure activities, 47
athletic, 45-46
conditioning activities, 47
confused with physical education, 64-65
consumer roles in, 50-51
dance as, 48
encouraging achievement in primary years, 72-73
experiencing, in physical education curriculum, 55-58

facilitating achievement in the secondary years, 73-74
game, 46-47
gymnastic, 45
importance of coaches and referees to, 51
interface with physical education. *See* Physical education/sport interface
organized competitive activities in, 45-47
place in physical education curriculum, 39
potential for cross-curricular links, 68
recognizing talent in, 65-66, 74
role and importance of, 44-45
typology of, 45-48
valuable experiences offered by, 67, 68
as a valued cultural form, 44-48
as a vehicle for physical education learning, 67
Sport and Young People: Partnership in Action, 71
Sport consumership, 50-51
Sport culture, 51-53
scholarship associated with, 53
Sport Examined, 144
Sport for All Charter, 45
Sport in Schools, 90
Sport/physical education interface. *See* Physical education/sport interface
Sports and Young People, 90
Sports Council, 45, 69, 76
Sports Leadership Award, 50
Sportslink scheme, 70
Sports studies, 146-147
Substitution model for physical education/ sport interface, 64-66
Superkids-Superfit exercise programme, 26
Swimmming, for children with severe learning disabilities, 127, 128

T

Target games, 44-45
Teacher preparation, 13
Teaching for understanding, 91-95
used to improve games teaching, 93-95
Team games, 11
Technical and Vocational Educational Initiative, 50, 70, 75, 138, 156
Training and Enterprise Councils, 150
Trois Rivières study, 27

V

Versus model for physical education/sport interface, 66-67
Vocational theme in physical education curriculum, 59